D1116451

Point of Departure

Other books by Ralph McAllister Ingersoll

In and Under Mexico
Report on England
America Is Worth Fighting For
Action on All Fronts
The Battle Is the Pay-off
Top Secret
The Great Ones
Wine of Violence

Point of Departure

An Adventure in Autobiography

by Ralph McAllister Ingersoll

Harcourt, Brace & World, Inc.   New York

To Harold W. Ross

CONTENTS

Part I

I · Concerning the Species *3*

II · Colin and Theresa Make a Family—Mine *13*

III · A New York Childhood *28*

IV · Teenager's Turnings *38*

V · Happy Time *50*

VI · It Takes All Kinds of Freshmen *62*

VII · Sophistication at Home   *82*

VIII · Educationally Speaking   *92*

IX · Sophistication Abroad   *108*

X · Ah, Love!   *122*

XI · In and Under California   *130*

XII · Greenwich Village in Brooklyn   *146*

XIII · The Sands Run Out   *156*

Part II

XIV · A Man Named Harold Ross   *163*

XV · Battle in William Street . . . and Other Encounters   *173*

XVI · The Makings of a Magazine   *185*

XVII · Dream's End   *205*

XVIII · And So to Matrimony   *212*

XIX · Manhattan Nightmare   *224*

XX · Gentlemen Pranksters All   *234*

XXI · And I Did   *241*

POSTSCRIPT   *245*

Part I

I · Concerning the Species

Like all free-blooded Americans, my parents were ancestor worshipers, and I heard a lot about my antecedents when I was a small boy.

Culturally, they told me, I am a half-breed—the result of the crossing of one line of American ancestors, predominantly puritan New England, with another, my mother's out of Savannah, Georgia. To this exogenesis, I attribute many psychological problems.

Of course, neither of these blood lines was really pure. The Northern branch was pure New England only in that its male Ingersolls had lived there continuously since the arrival of the first of them from Old England in the early 1600's. The marriages they made were with women from all over the lot. Starting in 1786, successive generations took as wives: a woman of Portuguese descent, a Dutch New Yorker, and the daughter of the most interesting character of them all, an upstate New Yorker named Zadoc Pratt.

Zadoc, my great-grandfather, was a nineteenth-century tycoon (in leather tanning) who had Character, Eccentricities, and four wives. Zadoc's daughter married Colin Macrae Ingersoll, who begat Colin Macrae Ingersoll, Jr., my father. I'll be back with more about Zadoc, for whom I was all but named; at the last moment, my mother put her foot down and just wouldn't have it—I'm kind of sorry to say.

I have less data on the McAllister half of me. That is because the Georgia McAllisters started a new slate, so to speak, when one of them made good in California in 1849. It was the Gold Rush that put him over, but as a lawyer rather than a miner. He sent some of the gold dust in which his fees were paid back to Georgia, and so financed the migration of the remainder of his family from Savannah to the West Coast, leaving family records behind them.

So I do not know what different cultural inheritances were mingled to produce the California McAllister who was my mother, Theresa, nicknamed Leta. In point of fact, the McAllister who may have most influenced my life contributed no genes at all to my inventory. His name was Ward McAllister, and he was my mother's uncle.

In his day, Ward McAllister was—"notorious" is the correct word. In some ways, he was a kind of nineteenth-century male Elsa Maxwell. Having appointed himself New York Society's social arbiter and party manager, par excellence, he made a good living out of it. Even so, he might have remained a small

potato but for his definition of Society as the "Four Hundred."
The newspapers of the day made such a big thing of this that
overnight he was, and remained, a national celebrity; almost a
century later, his phrase is still in use.

According to the original version of this episode, Ward early
in 1892 found himself in charge of a party to be given his friend
the Mrs. Astor, in her grand ballroom. Large as the ballroom
was, it could still not accomodate all those who were on this good
lady's list. So Ward undertook to cut the list down—to the four
hundred the ballroom would hold. Word of the pruning got
around, and McAllister is supposed to have boasted in some
club that it was a matter of small concern because "there are
only four hundred people in New York Society, anyway." That
did it—and from then on he was made—for who but Ward himself could state with authority which of New York's million and a
half inhabitants were either in or eligible for consideration by
the "Four Hundred"?

The character who so imposed himself on his contemporaries
was the subject of much debate in my family. He died in 1895—
five years before I was born—but my father, a grown man in
Ward's heyday, had vivid (and unpleasant) memories of him.

Ward was born in Savannah, had made a brief appearance in
New York when he was twenty—that would be in 1847—and
then had followed his father and brothers to California. But the
charm of pioneer life there escaped him, and he returned east
alone, arriving in New York in 1852 with only his wits to help
him. His defenders—even *he* had them—were later to assert
that he brought a fortune in California gold back with him, but
nothing in Ward's papers confirms this; nor did he marry money.

Ward's own story of how he got his start concerns somebody's
fancy-dress ball to which he was lucky enough to get an invitation. On the day the invitation arrived, he received word that
he had inherited the vast sum of one thousand dollars. One
thousand solid silver dollars in 1847 was the equivalent of three
or four thousand now. It was a small fortune. But Ward blew

the whole business on a costume for the fancy-dress ball, making himself so conspicuously elegant that "Society gasped."

At the time of the ball, Ward was "putting up" with a maiden relative on Stuyvesant Square who he hoped would leave him money. She didn't, but Ward managed—probably, in the beginning, with some assistance from his prosperous brothers on the West Coast. Within a few years, however, he was doing much better than "managing"; he had a house of his own in New York, a farm in Newport, and spent a good deal of his time hobnobbing with royalty in Europe. My father had no doubts whatever about how all this was accomplished. Ward, he snorted, "took money" —money or, better still, stocks and bonds from those whom he sponsored.

Ward's were the days when the first fortunes that had been made in the West were coming back to New York to be cashed in for something called "Social Acceptance"—a never very clearly understood commodity, but one considered highly desirable. These fortunes, amassed by males, were now for the first time under female management, and the competition among the ladies was intense. A Ward McAllister today would be an anachronism, but in the last half of the nineteenth century he was more ahead of his time than behind it. He saw himself as a civilized influence, teaching manners to the barbarians, and he died well pleased with himself.

His funeral, at Grace Church, on Broadway at Tenth Street, brought out so many of the curious that police reserves had to be called to restore order. It was quite an affair. The "Dead March" from *Saul* was rendered by eight French horns, two tubas, and eight trombones.

Ten years after his death, the august New York *Times* was still editorializing about him. "The death of Ward McAllister," and I quote, "forces attention for a moment upon the singular function which he assumed and performed for the society of New York. . . .

"In every modern society people are constantly coming to the front with money, and their social aspirations are sat in judgment upon by the people in possession. In monarchial society this was done by recognized officials. . . . The Prince of Wales is ex-officio leader. . . . It is openly and frequently charged that the Prince has taken money from aspiring persons for taking a lenient view of their claims. . . .

"It is at least evident that in a republican society where social differences are unsusceptible of scientific definition, somebody who . . . had tact enough . . . and was also willing to enforce his perception, had the power of fulfilling a very valuable social function. . . .

"He made so few mistakes none are remembered against him."

What Ward did to the family in which I grew up was to give it a kind of mild social notoriety for which it had no economic base. We were all ticketed by being related to him. The connection was made even closer by the fact that my mother had come east in the first place as Ward's protégée. She had been orphaned as a child and brought up in California by another uncle. This uncle had passed her on to Ward as soon as she was a grown young woman, and she was on the town as Ward's niece for some years before she met and married Father. Lord knows where they did meet, because Father was by no means the Ward McAllister type.

Ward would have done much better by his niece if she had co-operated, but Mother was a high-spirited, self-willed kind of girl who never thought twice about throwing over one of Uncle Ward's millionaire friends. Although she ended by marrying a young civil engineer from the provinces, she never quite lost the taste she acquired under Ward's tutelage, a taste for doing things in the grand manner, and for gaiety for gaiety's own sake. For Mother, life was always fun.

If my mother's standards were often those of her Uncle

Ward, my father was more apt to choose those of his grandfather Zadoc Pratt. This was a real tribute to the strength of Zadoc's strain; the pre-Zadoc Ingersoll tradition had been one of languid gentility—education in the law and the snagging of minor political plums.

When I was in college in New Haven, I ran into an ancient Swedish janitor who had known my grandfather Ingersoll. "My, he was a grand old yentleman," the janitor told me. "Everyone in New Haven knew him. Never did nothing all his life but walk around in a top hat!"

The grand old yentleman's father (for whom I was named) had once been Minister Plenipotentiary to Russia, and I was brought up on a jingle dedicated to him by his political opponents:

> Here's to Ralph the Ambassador spreading his sail
> To catch the first waft of the popular gale.
> He was hard up for Adams and hard down for Clay
> And steady for nothing but office and pay.

Zadoc's comment on Ralph's career would have been even harsher. Zadoc had begun *his* life as a cobbler's apprentice, sleeping under his master's bench and working as many hours as there were of daylight. He ended it as a master himself, of all he surveyed—which was a town in the Catskills, every building of which he had either built or caused to be built, and which, naturally, he named Prattsville.

In its heyday, Prattsville had a population of over a thousand. Most of the men worked in Zadoc's tannery and regularly voted to send him to Congress as their Representative. His four wives—two sets of sisters—he buried side by side under identical headstones, reserving a place for himself, as was proper, at the head of the formation.

Zadoc was a man of iron eccentricity. He loved horses, for instance, but would never ride upon or drive behind one that was not gray in color. Of some he was so fond that, when they died, he buried them in considerably more style than he did his wives. On *their* tombstones, the horses had their likenesses carved in bas-relief.

As a nineteenth-century tycoon, Zadoc had his own bank, of course, and printed his own money with his own picture on it. He built the bank on one corner of his front lawn, so situated that he could always keep an eye on it, even on the rare occasions when he lay abed. Eventually, even being separated by the width of the lawn bothered him, and he had the bank picked up and backed around until it could be tacked on to the main mansion itself. Thus it became a kind of anteroom to his own chamber and he could pop out of bed and through the back door of the bank, in his nightshirt, if he wanted to.

He also had very decided theories on how a bank should be run, and one of them was that the banker who had to rely on collateral should not be allowed to lend money. It was up to the banker to judge the borrower by looking at him. Zadoc could almost always tell an honest man—though there was one notable exception. Zadoc once staked a young itinerant land speculator who was passing through Prattsville, and became so intrigued that he made him a partner in one of his smaller tanneries. The bright young man ended by easing Zadoc out of the business and taking it over himself. His name was Jay Gould, and don't think Zadoc ever forgot it.

Zadoc forgot few things. This is my first autobiography, but before Zadoc was through with his life, he wrote half a dozen, printed at his own expense and bound with the best leather he tanned. And he was a good tanner and had a lot of medals, won in international competitions all over Europe, to show for it. From this you must not conclude that Zadoc was a complete egoist. He had his modest side. Several of his works about himself he attributed to others, labeling them biographies.

Besides being a writer, Zadoc was also a persistent patron of the arts. What is now called the Hudson River school included the work of itinerant painters who wandered up the valley from

New York and took commissions, usually to do family portraits. Often they carried with them an inventory of bodies, male and female, to which they had only to add the face of their latest subject.

Zadoc, however, would have none of the mass-produced work of these wandering artists. Instead, he put them to work doing landscapes of his beloved valley, panoramas of the town, and close-ups of his tanneries. For each and every one of these canvases he posed himself as well. It is the hallmark of a genuine Hudson River school painting from Prattsville that in the foreground there stands a symmetrical hemlock tree, under the branches of which sits Zadoc, his stovepipe hat either on his head or close beside him.

Zadoc never allowed himself to be painted except under a hemlock tree because, as he explained, "A hemlock tree is the source of my fortune." In those days, the first step in tanning leather was to find a hemlock tree, strip its bark, and boil this to extract the tannic acid. Zadoc was no man to turn his back on the origins of his wealth: natural resources and honest toil. The next work of art he subsidized was to drive this home even more forcibly.

One day the succession of itinerant painters was broken by the arrival of a sculptor. He may have had in mind doing a bust, but Zadoc saw a larger future for him. Prattsville, which straddles the Schoharie kill, is abutted on the north side by a high cliff of solid slate. About two thirds of this cliff is tree-covered, but toward the summit the slate finally takes over and rises in a solid rock wall thirty or forty feet high. On this, Zadoc put the sculptor to work—and there he must have labored for many a long year carving Zadoc's own anticipation of the Mount Rushmore Memorial in the Black Hills country of South Dakota. The results can still be seen by tourists who have lost their way in the Catskills. Prattsville is now a score of miles off any main highway, and the rail spur, for which Zadoc had done the grading, was never built. But the descendants of Zadoc's tannery hands still clear the paths up Pratt Rock, and show it proudly to summer visitors.

One of the first things that Zadoc had carved up there was the right arm of a son of toil, biceps bulging, elbow bent, and fist holding a hammer. (In the nineteenth century this was not considered subversive.) Next there are facsimiles of the tanneries—long shedlike affairs. And finally, of course, Zadoc himself rises, lantern-jawed, with long sharp nose and stern high forehead.

On Pratt Rock there is also the profile of Zadoc's only son, George, who took a ball in the chest trying to get his regiment through Stonewall Jackson's lines in the second Battle of Bull Run. Only one of his four wives bore Zadoc issue; these were George and my grandmother Julia.

There are lots more stories about Zadoc: about how every spring, into his seventieth year, he drove over to the Hudson at Catskill and swam the river from one side to the other the day the ice went out, just to prove to himself that he could still do it; about how it amused him to humiliate a laggard worker by taking him off the tannery's production line and commissioning him to spend the day catching grasshoppers for Zadoc to use as bait. The poor lad always thought this a fine idea—until he discovered that the receptacle provided by Zadoc was a wide-mouthed tin can with no top to it and Zadoc had told him to bring it back only when full! Zadoc records how non-laggards laughed when the faster the lad popped the grasshoppers in, the faster they popped themselves out, until the chap who'd been so anxious to avoid doing an honest day's work "threw down the hateful can and ran shamefacedly away."

Early in the twenties, my father and my uncle George decided that the Pratt homestead (which they had inherited) was too expensive to keep up, and sold it. It is still there, however, right on Main Street. Its façade of columns two stories high is still intact, although in need of a little fresh paint. The present owner lets out rooms, I think.

To me, the most dramatic evidence of the passage of time in Prattsville is the sawed-off stumps of the rotted elms that once separated the lawn from the sidewalk. They are easily four or five feet across. Zadoc put them in as seedlings.

You can readily see how having such highly flavored characters as Zadoc and Ward in my background influenced my childhood. Whenever I showed any ambition, Zadoc got the credit; whenever I stayed out too late, Ward McAllister took the blame. My own conclusion on the subject was that what I had really inherited was a headache: the problem of how to reconcile, within myself, the dominant characteristics of these divergent lines. Clearly they were at war within me.

What made the whole business more difficult was that although Father and Mother were married to each other for twenty-one years, neither ever wavered in his or her tribal loyalty, nor, while each was able, ceased subtly to proselyte their only son.

II · Colin and Theresa Make a Family—Mine

I have written of my father as if he owed his whole personality to his maternal grandfather Pratt, but that's not literally true. He thought of himself, first of all, as an Ingersoll, a Connecticut Ingersoll; "Connecticut" as distinct from "Philadelphia." The original American family, out of Salem, Massachusetts, had migrated as far as New Haven when it broke in two over issues

raised by the Revolution. The loyalist branch moved to Philadelphia, where it still flourishes, very much intact as a Family.
In cousins umpty-umph times removed, there is still a recogniz-
able family resemblance; both lines still throw large males with
prominent noses. The Philadelphia Ingersolls cohere, hang on to
both their money and their status as a Family; five successive
generations have been lawyers. The Connecticut Ingersolls, of
whom there had once been seven successive Jonathans, and who
had played reasonably prominent roles in colonial New England,
never seem to have found each other's company so congenial,
and there has been more New England individualism in their
tradition.

If you had asked my father who the Ingersolls were, he would
have answered, with some surprise at your asking such an obvious
question: "Gentlemen!" That is what made my father interesting as a character. He was fastidious to the point of eccentricity
about his person—and his costumes, for he was almost a dandy—
but his life's work was in the rough-and-tumble world of railroad
and bridge construction, and his voice was modulated to barking
orders to hunkies. While his manners were so courtly as to be
old-worldly, his viewpoint was one of progressive faith in action,
almost for action's sake. To him, an idler was a bum, however
well born; but he thought so much of "breeding" that he spared
the time for research into his own genealogy even when he was
sixteen-hours-a-seven-day-week active, which he always was
when one of his bridges was nearing completion.

This, plus the fact that he was past forty when I was born,
made him an awesome if shadowy figure to me when I was a
small boy. He was gentle and considerate in his manner toward
me (when he was around, which wasn't often), and unbending as
steel in the standards he set for me.

With molding me into a "gentleman," he hardly concerned
himself. I think he simply took for granted that, as his son, I
couldn't be anything else. But he took training me to be effective
very seriously. Tenacity and the use of ingenuity to solve one's

problems were held up to me above all other virtues except honesty, which *always* came first. "Stick-to-itiveness" and advice to "use your head, boy, use your head" were his preachments. As a child I was never able really to please him with my performance in either of these departments, although I was obviously too petrified to be less than reasonably honest.

Also, he was a perfectionist, and small boys' performances are never perfect. To this day, I wince from a fly rod because father's disappointment was so bitter when I failed to meet his standards as a fly-fisherman. He was more skillful than the pros who put on exhibitions at the annual Sportsman's Show in the old Madison Square Garden, able to run out a tapered trout line for hundreds of feet, upstream under brush hardly the height of a man above the surface of the water. This miracle he achieved by flipping the trout line into successive running loops, each of which moved the fly itself so many feet farther upstream.

The hands he used in these manipulations were at once large and finely made, with fingers as long and delicately shaped as a musician's. They were at the ends of very long arms attached to a once-ramrod-straight frame over six feet two inches in overall height.

I am seeing him again as I saw him as a child. His head was large—it seemed huge to me—its principal features being a commanding Roman nose, very clear and very blue eyes, and great sweeping mustaches, which were waxed when he was a young beau, then handlebar, and later majestically drooping. He was, as the Irish maids would have put it, a fine figure of a man.

He scared hell out of me—an unhappy circumstance of which he was blandly and totally unconscious. My further reaction, even as a small boy, was to be inordinately curious about him. What kind of a man was he, deep down inside? What had his life been before I found myself a part of it? Years later, a generation of years later, when we were finally friends, I tried to find out, but he never could tell me. He was inarticulate about himself, partially because it had simply never occurred to him to question either the values he lived by or the world in which he found himself. He had never really thought about either.

The last half of the nineteenth and the early years of the twentieth century belonged, in America, to the engineer and the builder—and Father was both. It was the era of peaceful co-existence between the American philosophy of optimism and the eternal reality of man's inhumanity to man. Mark Twain was its prophet, before the cynicism of his old age set in. Only reason and sound engineering principles need be applied and all the agonizing problems that had beset our ancestors would soon, and inevitably, disappear. Father believed that so implicitly that it never even occurred to him that he did. And being a Gentle-man and an Ingersoll made it equally unnecessary even to think about any problem involving personal behavior. Happy, happy day!

Nevertheless, I did, in my research into Father's life, come upon plenty of evidence that he did have problems to solve, even if he was unconscious of them. The first was his break with the purely genteel tradition of his Ingersoll forebears to become a scientific, rather than a law, student and, eventually, a construc-tion engineer.

As a boy, growing up in the old Ingersoll house on Trumbull Street in New Haven, which still stands, though it now belongs to Yale University, he was already showing characteristics not purely genteel Ingersoll. He was an expert rifleman, clever in the woods, and an enthusiastic naturalist.

Father was also, by his teens, something of a wag, and a minor sensation for his ingenuity. The two traits combined once to make an epic anecdote—itself suggestive of conflict between the genteel and the progressive in Father.

It began with his putting together his own homemade telegraph system. He had gotten the idea from old Samuel F. B. Morse, the portrait-painter-turned-inventor, who was a lifelong friend of my father's father. The idea spread, and soon half a dozen of Father's cronies had telegraph instruments, too, linked together with wire strung from house to tree to house. All the boys in Father's circle could then communicate in dots and dashes.

At this juncture, a young lady applied for membership in the club. She wanted to be in on what the boys said to each other. Most members were against this, but Father obliged. Instead of providing her with a telegraph key, however, he put together a box full of wires and gears, and, cutting out the front, he inserted a mirror in its place. This contraption Father solemnly installed in the young lady's boudoir, hitching it to wires leading to his house. This done, he announced that he had invented an improvement on the telegraph, an electric device by which you could actually transmit sight over the wires. When the young lady sat in front of the mirror, Father assured her, she would be entirely visible to him half a mile away.

Then all hell broke loose. A horrified family covered the obscene thing with bedclothes and cut the wires, and my father from their daughter's calling list. So you can see that Jules Verne was not the only man in the nineteenth century able to make an inspired guess as to what the twentieth might produce. But in the 1870's, this story so amused New Haven that Father's hoax made the local paper, and his former girl friend never quite recovered from the humiliation of having been so gullible as to believe television possible.

Father was still in high spirits when he matriculated in Yale Sheffield Scientific School to study civil engineering. Here the evidence comes from voluminous scrapbooks, which became mine only after his death at the age of eighty-nine. He must have thought them improper reading for the young, because he had kept them hidden most of his life. It is hard to say exactly why, unless it was for the clippings that told of Father and his fraternity brothers being turned out of their chapter house for having been caught entertaining young ladies there.

Even this affair shouldn't have been too scandalous, because Father's drawings of the young ladies themselves always showed them bodiced and bustled, and usually hatted, too, and carrying parasols. He was an excellent draftsman, drawing with a hard pencil in very fine lines, and he had a flair for likeness. Curiously, after his undergraduate days he was not to draw again until he was in his seventies. By that time a promising career as an artist was cut short by his failing eyesight, though not until the local gallery had put on a one-man show of his work. An eccentricity of both his early and his late work was that he never cared to draw anything except pretty girls. He was quite frank about this.

I came only gradually to understand the lighter side of Father's character, for evidence of it had been suppressed by the time I came along. When his college days were over and he went to work as a surveyor for the New York, New Haven and Hartford Railroad, it must have been with the savagest of intensity; for when he finally did become a civil engineer, Father turned out to be almost an infant prodigy. He was only twenty-six when the railroad made him Assistant to the President and responsible for double-tracking its main line between New Haven and Boston.

On that job, the Legal Department once told him he couldn't put the rails where he wanted because the right of way overran a graveyard. They were afraid they could never get permission to move the bodies. But by the next morning Father had moved the cemetery whole, headstones and all, and set it up in business again a quarter of a mile from its original location. So skillfully was the operation performed that no one ever did catch on.

This resourceful fellow was hardly forty when he was named Chief Engineer, not only of the railroad, but also of the City of New Haven. Yet even that was only the beginning. In 1905, when he was forty-seven, the City of New York sent for him to supervise the building of its last two great bridges over the East River—the Manhattan and the Queensboro. His title was Chief Engineer of the Bridge Department. After finishing this job, he set up in business for himself as a consulting engineer, and presently surveyed for the federal government the railroad potential of the Territory of Alaska. After that he got the most important offer of his life—from the Czar of All the Russias, to modernize six thousand miles of the Trans-Siberian Railway, but he turned it down because it would have meant bringing his family up abroad.

The effect of all this successful activity was to solidify the confidence I've made so much of in Father's character.

And what of Colin Ingersoll, Gentleman, while all this was going on? Perhaps being so untypical only made him more formidable as a construction boss. Damn (never God damn) was his strongest profanity, although he did occasionally allow himself a scornful *"hell,* no" if some course that outraged him was proposed.

I've sometimes thought that the conflict of worlds he lived in did have the effect of alienating Father from the more clannish aspects of familydom. Toward relatives, important per se in the maintenance of family-group consciousness, Father was curiously cool. Cousins aplenty we had, but their company never seemed to be preferred. Although Father was, in his day, the head of the clan, family problems as such always seemed vaguely to annoy him. Cousin X's marital difficulties must have seemed pretty small potatoes to a man concentrating on spanning an important river with a mighty bridge.

One exception comes to mind, and I tell it for its own charm as well as for its contribution to a definition of the term "Gentleman" on which I have been so heavily relying. It concerns Father's being drawn into a problem involving not one, but two cousins, both Ingersolls.

The hero is a cousin-called-uncle named Frank, who married a cousin on the same side and thus arrived at a position from which he could out-Ingersoll all the other Ingersolls. He and his Ingersoll wife lived in the last of the great Ingersoll houses, a very beautiful three-story colonial brick structure well sited on a bend overlooking the Connecticut River about halfway between Hartford and the coast. Between the two of them, they had also inherited the best of the family silver and furniture, including a set of oval table and twelve chairs that had been made for one of their forebears by Duncan Phyfe himself. This was a showpiece; but there were many others in the same class, and the silver included quite a lot of original Reveres, the Ingersoll family and Paul's having been related.

The only trouble with Uncle Frank's and Aunt Lucy's situation was that by their middle age—in the 1920's—they'd used up the last of their modest inheritances and had no way to support either the house or themselves. Being a Gentleman, Uncle Frank of course had no trade; so Aunt Lucy had to keep them alive by selling things she baked and by taking in roomers. Several better-heeled relatives tried to help this deserving pair, but they were much too proud to accept handouts.

All the family were aware of this situation, and a great many of its female members made pilgrimages to this out-of-the-way spot on the expectation of being left at least the Duncan Phyfe. Finally my father could stand it no longer and sat Uncle Frank and Aunt Lucy down together to tell them that they had no choice but to sell the house and buy themselves some square meals with the proceeds.

"You *must* have had offers," Father said. "This is really a very beautiful house, even if you haven't been able to keep it up the way you like."

"Oh, but we *have* had offers," Uncle Frank remonstrated gently. "Indeed we have. But they were all for *much* more than the house is worth."

"But . . .?" Father asked in bewilderment.

"But for *more* than it's worth . . ." Uncle Frank expostulated. "We couldn't possibly sell. A Gentleman doesn't sell things for a profit, you know."

To the best of my knowledge and belief, that's a true story. They never did sell, and both Frank and Lucy died not long after, as gentle and as sweet and as charming as they had always been—and as undernourished. All the calling that the female relatives had done proved to have been in vain, for the heirlooms were left to a museum—where, of course, they should have gone, there being no one of Frank's caliber left to look out for them.

Father told me about Uncle Frank's gentility the way a worldly young priest might speak of a saint whom he knew was not up to emulating. For Father often bought and sold for profit himself, although usually through the then gentlemanly institution of the stock exchange. The hallmarks of his own gentility were personal modesty and a kind of hear-and-speak-no-evil morality—hear and speak no evil, but keep one eye open, to avoid even the appearance of evil. "Never close the door when you are alone in a room with a lady," he once advised me. "People might misunderstand."

Father projected this approach into a lifelong practice of avoiding even casual reference to what he described as "the unpleasant side of life." When some member injected an unpleasant note in the family conversation, Father simply rose and left the room. If circumstances suggested that the "unpleasant" conversation might continue for some time, Father arranged to stay away until he judged the subject would be exhausted.

Naturally, this made it rather difficult for children living under his roof to get down to cases with Father, since he could always label the subject you chose "unpleasant" and hence undiscussable. Arguments about the adequacy of allowances most definitely came under this heading. After all, they had to do with money, by definition an unpleasant subject, particularly when there is not enough to go around.

But he had a dry, whimsical sense of humor, and people still speak of him as having had "a twinkle in his eye."

I suspect the twinkle in Father's eye was a good deal brighter in his youth than when I knew him, but the wry humor never left him. A few hours before he died, when I asked him if he was comfortable, his answer was, "What else am I able to be now?" And the day before, he had said to the pretty young nurse, who had complained of being cold, "Then climb in here with me."

Having so positive a character, you would expect Father to have had a son either in his own image or in the reverse of it. This might have been but for Mother, who was as positive a character as he, and exerted an influence diametrically opposed. Almost everything Father stood for, Mother either stood against or was disinterested in.

Her concept of gentility was a cavalier's, and Father got no credit at all for his hard work and his tenacity. The inferential criticism was that a better man would not have had to work so hard, and with less work would still have been a better provider. Father's frugality, and his sense of responsibility toward providing for the family's future, came out as miserliness, verging on the mean. Moreover, I doubt if Ward McAllister's niece was vastly impressed by honesty for its own sake. And certainly Father's fine discriminations and exacting standards of personal conduct must have been a bore, for Mother breezed through life with all sails set, undisturbed by inconsequential things like crosscurrents or how the ship might pitch on a course she had chosen.

How she got that way is, of course, pure speculation on my part, for I was a child when she died; but I have confidence in my picture of her personality. She made so vivid an impression on her contemporaries that for many years after her death she remained a conversation piece.

To find her you have to start with her childhood in California, orphaned amongst a whole clan of McAllisters, a generation away from their migration west. The uncle who brought her up had been an officer in the army. The army post on which she had been a child was at Sausalito, then a frontier fort on the transcontinental railway, not far from the Nevada border. There she would have grown half army brat, half pioneer child.

San Francisco would have been the first city she saw, when it was still self-confident and openhanded, the new capital of the West. Several of her other uncles were doing well there and were very much part of the city's life. One had even had a street named for him.

By the time she reached San Francisco, Theresa McAllister was almost a grown young woman, a strikingly handsome brunette with very fair skin and bright blue eyes. She was already scatterbrained, gregarious, bounding with energy, and the darling of her kinfolk.

She must, then, have been a brisk breeze out of the West when Ward McAllister brought her to New York and introduced her to a society which in California she had been brought up to laugh at. The Californian McAllisters considered Ward's life to be foolish as was Ward himself. He had been the sissy of the family, the one who had played with tea sets as a child. But whatever Ward may have been to New York, his niece was something new and vital, and she had such a wonderful time and enjoyed herself so mightily that she was in a fair way to become a perennial by the time she decided, at the age of twenty-nine, to marry Father. She had been around for almost a decade.

Mother was considered not very bright, but she was effective. The first thing she did as soon as she began bearing her new husband children was to free herself from the chore of bringing them up. This she accomplished, and without funds, by converting a teen-age Irish girl into her slave and alter ego. The Irish girl's name was Annie McCabe, and Mother adopted her without benefit of papers—"absorbed" would be more the way it was. Annie's services had first been engaged at the age of eleven, "to help the ladies lay off their coats at parties." This led to her employment as what we would call a baby sitter; the term then was "a walker," one who walked babies in their perambulators. After she came to live with us, the concept of employment was abandoned, and Annie was simply fed, clothed, and given spending money—grudgingly.

That was in the early 1890's; in the late 1940's I buried her. In between those years, Arny, which was my name for her, had never had a thought but for Theresa McAllister's family, to whom she had given her whole life. I have never known a purer love than hers. It was Mother's genius to inspire that kind of loyalty.

With the children safe in Arny's capable hands, Mother could again devote herself to being merry. The word "merry" is carefully chosen, because it is the one most often used about Theresa by her contemporaries. She did not make merry; she simply *was*. She was the kind of person who would be halfway through unpacking upon her arrival at a new base when the whole business would bore her and she would say, "Oh, let's have a party!" and send scurrying for guests to entertain amongst the packing boxes. She was a budgeter who would skimp on clothes, or even food, to shoot the works on a trip to Europe; the kind of housekeeper who didn't care a hang about upstairs if the parlor was presentable.

Mother's only real traits in common with Father were her energy and her ingenuity—and she needed both in abundance to keep the kettle boiling. A civil engineer's salary was hardly adequate to support life in the grand manner, or to entertain in the style to which Ward had accustomed her. Mother never let that bother her. Once when she needed a ball gown which there was no money to buy, she simply pulled down her best portieres and had Arny run up the material into a creation. It was the talk of the affair. Another time (*Town Topics* recorded this one) Mother's guests were already arriving for high tea when a maid had to inform her that there was no bread in the house. "It doesn't matter," Theresa is quoted as saying, "just serve them toast."

Inherited from the same stock, or acquired by association, there was a lot of Ward McAllister in his niece. If there were no means with which to take a social objective, she knew well the uses of both bluff and brass, but no one ever questioned either her charm or her courage. An even more striking resemblance lay in Theresa's and Ward's devotion to the same god: merriment for merriment's own sake. Theresa's children might fatigue her, but never a grand ball, a gay picnic, or even informal fun around the piano, which she played quite well. Her friends were legion, and it was a long time before she was forgotten.

What a weirdly wonderful creature she must have seemed to her New England husband, who was taking his career as a civil engineer so seriously. There is no doubt but that he adored her, and when she died, he traveled alone to France to find a roadside cross in Brittany that she had once admired. He had it reproduced in marble for her tombstone.

The family these two were to produce began a year after they were married, with my oldest sister, Theresa's arrival, ten years ahead of me. Then came Marion, who died of a burst appendix at six; and after her, a third female child. By now despairing of a son, they gave this one my father's name, tacking on an "e" to make it Coline. Once upon a time, I thought this act the theft of my birthright, and for years I referred to myself as Mac, in protest. Mac Ingersoll was what my father had been called by his intimates.

While the girl children were being born and growing up, Father was hurrying back and forth between New Haven and Boston, to which he was transferred by the railroad when he became Assistant to the President. In 1900, he returned to New Haven as Chief Engineer of the road—presumably for once and for all. At forty-two he had reached the top of his first ladder.

Despite growing encumbrances, Father had saved money enough to buy, out on Whitney Avenue, a house that must have fulfilled both their dreams. Solidly built of yellow brick, with slate roofs and copper flashing, it was an engineer's fortress; romantically gabled, it had also all the fittings of the period, including a porte-cochere and a turret-like tower, which had a miniature ballroom in it for entertaining. In this house I was born, and, because my room was beneath the tower, my earliest memories are of music and dancing over my head.

The family now had its male child and considered itself complete. It was to stay intact for a scant ten years, which Father in his old age must have looked back upon as the Days of the Empire. For the first five of them, he was the home-town boy who had made good and the master of a house everyone envied. It was presided over by a mistress who made it into a kind of salon for the most glamorous characters of the University which Father had attended, for its wittiest professors, its handsomest young instructors, and its football heroes. Mother enslaved them all.

Then, with the call from the City of New York, the New Haven days were over. The glamorous house on Whitney Avenue was shut up, and we moved down to a rented brownstone-front on East Seventieth Street opposite the old Presbyterian Hospital. And Mother was back at last in Ward's world, returned to the scene of her girlhood triumphs, but now as the wife of a prominent man and with three children of her own to introduce one day to Society. All of us were in new schools, with new playmates and a fascinating new city to explore.

But just as there began to seem no end to the beneficence of life—after the whole family had shared in the latest trip to Europe and a brownstone-front of our own had just been purchased—the end of it all came abruptly and without warning.

While I was still nine, Mother languished suddenly, and began, in her forty-ninth year, to waste away. There was a family story that an accident had caused the cancer. In her New Haven days, she had loved to ride in a tiny straw pony cart. Once, the animal that pulled it had run away and overturned the rig. She had been kicked in the belly trying to recover the pony.

The terrible decision my father had to make was whether to prolong Mother's life in horrid pain by sanctioning an operation the doctors said would be futile or simply to ease her

death, unscarred, with opiates. He chose the latter. He and
Arny ground the opium powder and compounded the pills
themselves, in a bathroom off the chamber where she lay. A
homemade canopy of barrel staves held the bedclothes from
her body, which now knew only pain. Her skin was so sensitive
to weight that it could not bear the touch of a sheet.

It took Mother almost a year to die, but her cheerful courage
never faltered. She spent her last months organizing, to the last
minute detail, the lives that her husband and children should
lead after she was dead. In the carrying out of her orders, Arny
was to be her principal instrument.

III · A New York Childhood

Mother died in the winter of 1910. Twenty-five years later, I began paying a psychoanalyst five thousand a year to advise me, in effect, on my reactions to this event. Actually, all I asked was: "How can anyone able to sit up and take nourishment be such a demonstrable idiot in matters emotional?" And what the psychiatrist replied was: "After I have helped you to answer that for yourself, you will exclaim, 'But I knew *that* all the time!' "

He was right—and what I had been unable to face was how

terribly in love I had been with my glamorous mother, and how bitterly rejected I had felt. Good old Oedipus complex—it never made any sense to me until I found I had one of my own!

Whether Mother and I would have worked it all out in happy harmony had her death not left our conflict unresolved, who can tell—and the purpose of this book is not to relive my analysis. But this much, it seems to me, has to be set down to explain the violence done my childhood by the whole relationship. On each of the first three anniversaries of Mother's death, I fell physically ill, and each year almost died—the first two of rheumatic fever and the last of scarlet fever. Write it off to coincidence if you will, but that's the way it was.

Up until Mother's death I had been a discontented, whining child, stuffed until I was bursting at the seams and spoiled (by Amy) to within an inch of my life. Scandalizing relatives, I clung to my nursing bottle until I was ten. My favorite diversions were braining people with tightly rolled newspapers and eating whole platefuls of butterballs, popping them into my mouth like marbles. In school I was known either as Fat or as Stinky, and a relative who visited during that period wrote years later to inquire, "Is little Ralph as disagreeable as ever?"

I was, of course, wholly unconscious of the effect Mother had had on me, and my only contribution to her funeral was to howl bloody murder because they wouldn't let me sight-see out of the window as our carriage followed the hearse. I could not get through my head why everyone made such a solemn business of it, and I have no memories of ever crying from grief.

But within a few years thereafter my whole personality, as well as the shape of my body, had changed radically. I turned suddenly into a skinny extrovert, the old nicknames were forgotten, and I became a leader in organized sports at school and of a gang of my own after hours.

You are at liberty to put all this down to normal glandular development; I am not trying to sell my interpretation but simply to record a striking change in behavior after my mother's death.

The house to which we moved after Mother's death—it was on Seventy-first Street—was the first home I remember clearly. I had a wonderful time there. I had not one, but two rooms of my own—cubbyholes on the fifth floor, where the maids lived. I called one my office. In it I was presently to build a workbench for explorations into chemistry and to set up a genuine two-way wireless transmitter (with a great sign lettered "DANGER, 10,000 VOLTS") with which I barely got an almost intelligible signal down to a fellow conspirator five houses away.

It was in these attic rooms that Arny nursed me patiently through my three unexplained spells of fever, and each year I had the summer in which to grow strong again at a camp Father had taken on Lake Winnipesaukee, in New Hampshire. After these years were past, I began to blossom in the small preparatory school to which I was consigned. It was called Mr. Kirmayer's Classes and was on East Sixtieth Street.

Mr. Kirmayer was as good a schoolmaster as I remember. Slim, handsome, ramrod-straight, he had a Prussian background (and a saber scar from Heidelberg), but he had also imagination not usually associated with Prussians. For instance, once a week the whole school—there were only fifty or sixty of us—spent an afternoon in a factory, seeing bread baked or paper boxes put together or watching some other such activity, to suggest to us that somebody had to make the money that was spent on Park Avenue.

For play, Mr. Kirmayer rented a vacant lot on upper Fifth Avenue, in the Nineties somewhere—there were plenty of them then—and we went there every afternoon. If you had your parents' permission, as I did, you went from school to The Lot on roller skates, up Fifth Avenue, hitching rides (if you could get away with it) on the brewery trucks that were still pulled by beautiful, big, and noisy horses. The noise they made was important, because it kept the driver from hearing your skates. By this time I had acquired very long legs, and when I was caught, I never had any trouble getting away unless a skate came off.

You could find lots of other ways to be a nuisance on roller skates then. A favorite dare was to slip into Bloomingdale's store through a Lexington Avenue entrance, skate through the whole of the ground floor and out on the Third Avenue side without a floorwalker being able to lay a hand on you. I can still recall this triumph with a feeling of warmth and a happy memory of fat ladies on their behinds with bundles scattered right and left. Don't let anyone tell you that a New York childhood, even on Park Avenue, can't be fun.

Take the matter of precision bombing with water bombs. If you know how, you can fold an ordinary piece of square paper into a virtually round bomb with an opening about as big as your little finger in the top. When this is done carefully, it will hold water for several minutes or more, depending on the quality of the paper. You simply hold the bomb under a bathroom spigot, transport it rapidly to a window, and drop it on the most eligible passer-by. In 1911 and 1912 on East Seventy-first Street, this was most rewardingly done on a Sunday morning. It was still the custom of heads of households to wear top hats to church then.

I had a pretty good task force for this kind of thing at one time, very formally organized and called "The XXX Club." We weren't always malicious. Once, we produced a play. I wrote and directed it myself, but modestly let another boy be the hero— the villain's part was so much better. He was conceived to be a Jekyll-and-Hyde character, a poor old blind man by day but able, and the world knew this not, to see perfectly by night. So gifted was he that by the play's opening scene he had established himself as a master burglar. This was the simple part of the plot. From there on, it got so complicated that not even the cast, let alone the audience, was able to follow the story.

One of my classmates, whose family was a lot wealthier than mine, had a house a block long on Park Avenue in the Sixties with an electric elevator leading up to an economy-size ballroom on the third floor. This particular building happens to be the Swedish Consulate now. We put on our play there, encouraged, but in no way aided, by Mr. Kirmayer and his assistants. Another classmate, who was considered an electrical genius, was in charge of bringing into existence a battery of genuine footlights. At the first performance, his crowning achievement was to blow out a crucial fuse, with the audience only half seated and a few of them still in the electric elevator suspended between floors. But somebody re-established the connections and we got off to a flying start.

My play was a very serious melodrama, with social overtones. But if the audience chose to take it as farce, that was perfectly all right with us. The only solid objective of all concerned was to play the thing through to a climax scene in which the blind burglar shot it out with the cops. At this stage, the entire cast, with each and every man equipped with a fifty-shot repeating cap pistol, had at each other. When the rolling gunfire went on and on, and on and *on*—past all theatrical liberty—tears began to stream down people's faces and some of them did actually fall off their shaky campstools and roll in the aisles with laughter. It was then that the assembled audience of relatives stood—to a man, woman, and pigtailed sister—to demand the repeat performance that we gave the following week. Our admission charge was twenty-five cents, and we did very well.

Despite such diversions, my life those years had its serious side. Somewhere along the line I had been badly bitten by the self-improvement bug. At twelve, I rather grimly doubted that I was being adequately educated at school. Too many hours in my days—which for some reason I was sure were numbered—were being wasted. So I set aside a period from four to seven every afternoon and opened up a school of my own at home. The subjects I chose to teach myself were typewriting, shorthand, and piano playing, in stints of one hour each.

The piano-playing part was a spite chore. After Mother's

death, it was agreed that my sisters should have musical educations, the eldest, Theresa, taking up the piano, and Coline the violin. These allotments apparently exhausted the family budget, and I was left out in the cold, understanding only that I was being deprived of a privilege considered special.

Most small boys would have danced with glee. Instead, I made a secret pact with myself to get even by learning to play despite them. To keep my project a secret, I would approach the piano only when there was no one else in the house. From a passing aunt, I learned the only fact about sheet music I considered essential: which key on the piano you were supposed to hit when the black dot is printed on the lowest of the five lines on the staff. I knew that when I had that one note placed, I had them all. The piece I chose to master was a popular ragtime job called "The Oceanic Roll." I was able to work out and memorize about a chord an hour. I had to do the right hand first, and then the left hand separately; then put the two together. It took me a whole winter of surreptitious study to accomplish this. But when I was through, I could play that piece, and that piece only, with vigor and even some rhythm.

All this effort led to a colossal triumph the following summer when I took over a party my sisters were attending at the country club. I had sneaked in the back way and come upon a roomful of male and female adults standing about waiting for the pianist to show up. In an inspired moment I leaped upon the stool, seized the keyboard, and broke into a rollicking "Oceanic Roll." My sisters, standing nearby, were bug-eyed with amazement, and I reached dizzying heights of satisfaction as a whole room of adults fell into each other's arms and began dancing. On and on I went, and round and round and round they went—and over and over, chorus after chorus, out came . . . "The Oceanic Roll." Finally a few couples stopped and applauded to get my attention, and someone yelled, "Play something else." When the whole room took up the cry, I leaped off the stool and fled in shame. For "The Oceanic Roll" was as far as my musical education had gone.

These sisters of mine were always a problem. One was ten years older and the other five. They were fourteen and nineteen when I was delivered into their hands, just grown up enough to take the mission of civilizing me very seriously. Lessons in table manners and deportment were now never-ending, and not even Arny could save me.

Coline, the younger of the two, was a gentle girl, anxious to be loved, and easily hurt. I could handle her, after a fashion. But Te was something else again. She was smarter than Coline and gifted with an uncanny instinct for knowing the vulnerable points in a small boy's armor. She knew, for instance, that the confiscation of a prized possession could hurt more than any lecture. And she was a natural-born disciplinarian.

Too bad that my sisters were so much older than I in those formative years. There are few age differences greater than that which exists between ten and fifteen. I would like to have been closer to them and to have known them better. Both grew up to be very pleasant women, and have led successful lives.

When I was a boy, I liked Coline better but admired Theresa more. Even I had to admit that Te was awfully good looking for a girl, and the gay life she led fascinated me. Those were the days when at grown-up parties they gave favors, and Theresa used to come home at daybreak with armfuls of them. Sometimes I was already awake when she came in, clattering upstairs followed by the faithful Arny, who had spent a night of it chaperoning her. Girls were never allowed anywhere without chaperones then, and a swain whose breath smelled of liquor was banished instantly and never asked back.

Sisters—schmisters! As I have said, mine were shadowy characters to me when I was a small boy. The personality that had real significance to me in my boyhood was Annie McCabe, on whom I have hardly touched. Annie McCabe, called Arny, and never anything else, was short, compact, already graying, and never dressed in other than a plain white shirtwaist and a box-like skirt, over which she wore a severely tailored coat when she went out into the world beyond our doors. Arny, with her Irish button of a nose in her plain Irish face, and the solemn, responsible expression she usually wore on it—Arny was my world when I was at home.

I can make out a case for my relationship with Arny's being the single most important influence in my whole life's pattern. It was she who was my true mother, in the sense that all the love that I experienced in my childhood came from her, and I absorbed her values naturally and unconsciously.

Arny's most outstanding characteristic was of warm tolerance of human frailty, but it sprang from so deep a well that it emerged without either the sentimentality or the sloppiness of the overtolerant. She had a snorting Irish scorn for stupidity, however understanding she was of it, and there was an equally solid common sense about the advice she gave for the solution of any problem. I suppose these are the racial characteristics that make the Irish such natural politicians, in the good use of the word. Many times I have thought that if Arny had been a man, she would have risen to a commanding position in the government of the land to which her parents had emigrated not long before she was born.

But tolerance and a dedication to common (as distinct from fancy) sense were not the things about Arny that made the most impression on her foster son. What did was her monolithic confidence that the family which had adopted her were pure, eighteen-carat Aristocracy. Her belief in the existence of an Aristocracy—and in the logic and rightness of the concept—had been bred into her through centuries in the old country. Her definition of an Aristocracy was, of course, her own, and was lived, rather than articulated.

An Aristocrat, naturally, had first to be born one. But if he was, he could do no serious wrong—only silly things which, if they were unworthy of his heritage, were best ignored. Moreover, if he was truly bred, his natural superiority would be self-evident. Instinctively, he would be at once kind, intelligent, and effective, sensitive to and thoughtful of others, and wholly without fear. He could also, by natural right, associate with anyone on terms of easy camaraderie—finding himself as at home (if less comfortable) in a hovel as in a palace. This was a function of his inborn superiority, which made it unnecessary for him to look down on any man, and impossible for him to look up. There was a godlike quality to Arny's Aristocrat, whose simplicity was the simplicity of greatness. It was her only romanticism.

The first words written about Arny and me were Mother's comment in my scrapbook; she kept one for each child. I was only a few months old, and the words were "Arny is his body servant and his slave." As I grew, family friends and relatives, observing, rarely failed to comment, in horror, on "the way Arny spoils that boy!" I would not leave her bed until almost as big as she, and if I have (and I do have) a curious way of pronouncing many words, it is because I heard them first when Arny read aloud to me. Long before I was ten, I made her plod through volume after volume of Stevenson and Dumas (from bound sets in the family library), hour after hour—for my word was law and I wanted "just another chapter" as much as any other little boy postponing bed.

How well I survived the "spoiling"—the letting me eat only what I pleased (meatballs, mashed potatoes, and butterballs), come and go as I pleased (I had my own house key at the age of eleven), and generally raise all the hell I cared to—whether these indulgences marked me for life only my sisters and wives can testify to.

What *I* recognize is the foundation of confidence—in life in general and in myself in particular—that Arny's confidence in my superiority gave me. At a very tender age, I was I, and an I born impervious in the soul to the slings and arrows of outrageous fortune. It was an inner arrogance that Arny would be after giving me, so deep that it never occurred to me that I could be really hurt by anyone's acts but my own. I was I, without need for further honor, or for riches for their own sake or any man's approval.

I would, of course, in some vague way be required to live up to myself, to live by standards unasked of lesser men, but if I was ever *too* tough on myself, there was always Arny's other philosophy—of tolerance—to fall back upon.

In the battle of values between Mother and Father, Arny was always on Mother's cavalier side. Once in my teens, when I first came home really stinking drunk, Arny put me tenderly to bed and stood over me as I closed my eyes sighing happily, "Drunk as a Lord, drunk as a real Lord!"

These words about Arny and what she stood for in my upbringing are written as a kind of afterthought. The narrative of my childhood done, and reread, I felt that something truly important wasn't there. It was Arny—Arny as an influence on me, rather than merely as a young girl whom Mother had taken advantage of. Arny's influence on me had simply been too all-embracing, too taken for granted, to have intruded itself when I was writing narrative.

With these paragraphs, I hasten to make amends. I was Arny's "boy," not Theresa McAllister's, when I was a child. I still am Arny's boy.

IV · Teenager's Turnings

It took a scant five years after Mother's death for her little family empire to fall apart and, in its crumbling, to make her son the nonconformist he has been ever since. As the twig is bent . . .

Until her death, the Ingersoll family was eminently orthodox, socially secure, and altogether coherent. It made sense. It was a member of New York Society, in first-rate standing. And New York Society with a capital S made sense, too, then. It was a kind of small village community, hidden away in (and from) the big vulgar metropolis that housed it. Within the invisible confines of this village, everyone knew everyone—as in the smallest village—and policed everyone else's behavior. Ostracism was the ultimate, and most terrible, punishment; and no one in the Ingersoll family would dream of courting it by failing to conform to Society's mores or by breaking its laws. At the same time, we children were made conscious of the fact that we belonged to a special group, however difficult it might be to define it, and that we had an obligation to conduct becoming that group.

The tale of my teens is the story of how it came about that I first tasted the forbidden fruit of unorthodox behavior and was, gradually and rather grudgingly, expelled from Eden. There is little that is heroic—or naughty or even gay—about it. I did not elope in my teens with the Wrong Woman or cheat at cards. And by nature, as I think I have found out, I am essentially an orthodox man and a respecter of Christian ethics. It was rather that, as a boy, a series of circumstances far beyond my control swept me out of the main stream and into the eddies. There I was so spun about that I had no choice but to adjust myself to nonconformity and points of view originally alien in order to survive.

And that adjustment has stayed with me all my life. It is real but has never been quite complete. I am still at home, and feel warmed, when I am among the kind of people I grew up with. But the good feeling doesn't last. I am soon uncomfortable again, as they made me feel when I was a boy in my teens. And I want, again as I wanted then, to get out and away from them to lead my own unorthodox—sometimes uncomfortable, but more often satisfying—nutty kind of existence.

Looking back, it is easy enough to see how it happened—and how inadvertently. With a little bit of luck and ten cents' worth of common sense the family that wanted their only male offspring to be an orthodox McAllister-Ingersoll could have had me that way —for whatever purpose would be another story. But they had neither the wit nor the luck.

Item 1: Mother's death upset the balance of power in the classic American battle for control of the family budget. Without the cavalier in Mother, the puritan in Father took over. After her death, money was only spent sensibly, except for a few skirmishes won by Theresa in the interest of her wardrobe. Effects on the male heir apparent: instead of being sent away to St. Paul's, in Concord, New Hampshire, at the age of twelve, with my fellows, I was kept at home. I went on attending Mr. Kirmayer's classes for reasons of economy. (I had, of course, literally been entered at St. Paul's since about the time I was christened.)

Also, I was no longer dressed "in fashion." I outwore, as well as outgrew, cheap clothes; nor were the starched stiff collars of my father's day replaced, about my neck, by the less formal wear that succeeded them. I was out of uniform as well as out of step. If this appalls sensible grownups as too picayune to be taken seriously, teenagers will understand me.

Item 2: When I had outgrown his regular classes, Mr. Kirmayer kept me on by improvising instruction through high-school levels. Thereby I was more tutored than classroom-taught. Being a bright boy, and furiously energetic, even with one hand tied behind my back I went through a slow-paced curriculum so rapidly that by my fifteenth year I had taken and passed all but one or two of my college entrance board examinations. They were a cinch! With a summer more of tutoring, I would have been in a position to enter Yale before my sixteenth birthday.

Result: Sheer horror was my sisters' reaction! Taking a three-year course at Yale, I might be graduated at *eighteen!* To be *finishing* college when most correct young men were *entering* . . . why I would be a freak!

Ridiculous? Implausible? Please believe me that in 1915, in the little village that was my New York, having a precocious son was an appallingly close call with catastrophe. My sisters, by then grown young women, rallied to save me—and their own reputations—from my bewildered father. Bereft of Mother's good sound social values, he might have succumbed to his engineer's logic and even encouraged me. He was very proud of my being a bright son. But my older sisters' last effective act before leaving the sinking family ship was to persuade him to "hold the boy back" until he is "old enough to get something out of going to college" —something besides wholly unimportant book-learning, that is.

Chain reactions: First, an unsuccessful revolt—which we will get to in due time. For present purposes, I will only record that it exposed me to the working unwashed for two most formative summers, and brought me quickly back to attend, at long last, an orthodox prep school for a long and bitter school year.

The prep school eventually chosen was Hotchkiss, in the township of Salisbury, Connecticut, where my father, having meanwhile remarried, now took up residence. At first I was even a day boy, than which there was nothing lower. Again, we will come to my reaction to that.

Father's remarriage was most surely Item 3 in the process of my expulsion to the limbo of the nonconformist. For my new stepmother was (a) herself a nonconformist of sorts, who (b) promptly upon marrying my father persuaded him to retire from active life. He soon sold the family homestead in New York and retired to live a rural life in Connecticut's Litchfield County.

With the introduction of my stepmother, whom I called Tante (pronounced Tanta), it is time to get back to my narrative. If I were to continue ticking off the influences that one day were to banish me even from the social register, I would have to go on through the thwarting experiences of World War I, Yale University as I found it when, at a more orthodox seventeen, I finally matriculated, and the psychological turns by which I became a mining engineer. But this would throw even my rambling reminiscence out of step.

So let me go back to the breaking up of the top-drawer family that Mother had kept together until her death at 44 East Seventieth Street in New York City in the month of March in 1910.

For a long time after Mother's death it had been still-pond-no-more-moving, with all our lives immobilized by her dead hand.

Life was run by the gospel of Your Mother as interpreted by
Saint Arny. Father was allowed the consolation of working
harder than ever building bridges, but could be permitted no serious social life of his own lest he fall into the hands of "some
woman"—whose influence might threaten the sanctity of Mother's
memory. My sisters, too, had to toe the line, and their friends
were limited to families of whom Mother would have approved.

Theresa was the first to break away, to marry not one of her
perennial beaux from New York's better clubs, but a roughneck
ten years her senior and self-made. He was a genitourinary sur-
geon from Boston whose joke that his trade was plumbing didn't
amuse Father.

Then it was Father's turn to fall into the hands of an outlander
—that is, someone Mother hadn't known—a handsome maiden
lady of forty summers. Her name was Marie Harrison, and,
despite my sisters' objections, her credentials were eminently in
order. She had led a highly respectable if slightly too busy life,
the unorthodox feature of which had been a brief period as the
editor of *Vogue*. A man named Tunure had married her sister and
started *Vogue,* and she had gone to work for him. When he died
suddenly, he left her in charge.

Marie must have been an extremely handsome young woman—
and a somewhat confusing one, because she made no secret of the
fact that she had never been moved by male charms. Her alliance
with my father had all the earmarks of being founded principally
on mutual respect, and the first sales talk I got from Father on the
subject began, "You will like her, boy. She thinks like a man."

However, whether Marie was or was not the right second wife
for my father was beside the point. My father's decision to marry
anyone was lese majesty to Mother's Memory, and Arny and my
sisters would have none of her. For two years they waged a
guerrilla war of innuendo and unkindness. But by 1916, Marie
had won. My father married her, almost surreptitiously, in an
inconspicuous Episcopal church we had never attended—and the
old order was over.

Early in this campaign, I had aligned myself on Father's side, and perhaps I was at last some comfort to him. It was a labor of love on my part, for I was continually being pressed into service as a chaperon on the dullest possible Sunday excursions into the spring woods of Westchester or across the river to climb the Palisades. Father and Tante were die-hard nature lovers, and their idea of a good thing to do on an April Sunday was to look for crocuses. At fifteen, it wasn't mine.

Back in Seventy-first Street, Tante was now installed, the titular head but as yet unprivileged to move a piece of furniture.

I surveyed my life and found it seriously wanting. So, with the household still preoccupied with the problems of its readjustment, I hit my father with my big idea. Not only was I *not* going to Yale—which had been taken for granted for me—but after this year I was through with schools of any kind. Along about February, I announced that come spring I was leaving home.

Whether I had caught Father in a weak moment—he had still to be grateful to me for my moral support of his remarriage—or whether it was because it never occurred to him to take me seriously, I have no idea; but his handling of my rebellion was magnificent. He simply said, "Certainly! I'll start lining up a job for you now."

And he did. It was in the spring of my fifteenth year that I reported for work with a construction gang in Fairfield, Maine, to be employed at the sum of forty dollars a month as a rodman for the surveyors. With the job went free bunk space along with the others in a building that had been condemned along the right of way. The construction gang was building a bridge over the Kennebec River for the Maine Central Railroad.

I have used the rather strong word "magnificent" for my father's gesture. This is in admiration of the ease with which he succeeded in getting his way with a teen-ager. What he wanted, and it seemed desperately important to him, was to make me into a civil engineer, for which, of course, a college education was essential. By apparently giving in to my first rebellion, he won half the struggle; by farming me out as the lowest-paid member of an engineering crew, he won the other half.

I hadn't been at work a week before I caught on to the fact that all the money I could ever get holding a rod somebody looked at through a transit was forty dollars a month. Yet in my new world there was no promotion until I learned to run the transit myself. Father never even had to explain that to me.

Nor did I have to be nudged into the conclusion that life at Yale University might not be so bad after all, in contrast with life in the uppermost of three springless bunks in a bunkhouse inhabited by sophisticated male animals who found my innocence the best joke they'd run into in years. When for the first two days I asked too many questions about my job, they spent the next two weeks hazing me with a hailstorm of questions about my private life and natural functions. As low man on the totem pole, I had every errand to run for every man Jack of them. It wasn't such an awfully long time, despite the glamour of being on my own and wholly self-supporting, before I was scrambling in panic for some philosophy with which to console myself. Admitting that life was never so good as it promised to be, when, oh, when, would it cease being as bad as it seemed now?

It was the girl who played the piano in the nickelodeon who got me out of that first crisis. I might never have survived if it had not been for Marjorie Webber.

Marjorie was eighteen or nineteen and a strikingly good-looking girl. She was also untouchable, inviolate, and unapproachable, because she was a judge's daughter, and the word was out that the judge would brook no nonsense when he let his daughter play the piano at the movie house Saturday nights. So, since girls were scarce in a small town suddenly flooded with several hundred steelworkers and construction roustabouts, the first ten rows of the movie were jammed each Saturday with scrubbed and

unnaturally respectful males watching, not "The Perils of Paul-
ine," but the even-harder-to-trap Marjorie Webber. And, afterward, as she sipped her soda alone at the drugstore counter, the
gang clustered at the far end of the room, devouring her every
gesture.

What in the world emboldened me I'll never know. I was
acutely shy of girls in those days. But one Saturday night I just
up and detached myself from the gawkers, walked solemnly
over to where she sat, and said, "Hello." And the next thing
I knew—to my own as well as everyone else's amazement—we
were pals, and I was being asked home to dine at the table over
which the judge himself presided. The day after this revelation
of my unsuspected prowess, I could for the first time consider
the bunkhouse my home. I was a man among men, by courtesy
of my conquest of Marjorie.

I wish I had a lot more to say about my relationship with
Marjorie herself. As far as that affair went, I sailed under the
falsest of colors among my fellow males. The less I was in-
clined even to mention her name in the bunkhouse, the more
was suspected, and presently vouched for by liars-in-their-teeth.
A lion amongst these wolves, with Marjorie I remained a very
timid lamb. And the lamb's only success was to make life more
difficult for himself by pretending to be twenty and a college
man. Marjorie was very nice about not probing the weak points
of my story, and we spent most of many pleasant hours together
talking about religion. If the boys at the bunkhouse had ever
found out . . .

What my release from torment meant to me on the job was
that for the first time I could take stock of it. The bridge we were
building was, for its time and place, an ambitious one, a long
curving succession of steel spans balanced on tall concrete piers
rising from the river bed. It was really a beautiful bridge, and I
should have been impressed. But the unpalatable truth that I
now discovered was that it had been ordered from a catalogue.

As civil engineers, my crew's only function was to set out the stakes that showed where the component parts were to be placed. It wasn't nearly so complicated as putting something together with a Meccano set. Diligent questions, now answered, unmasked this plot, and it was a disillusionment from which I never recovered.

But neither was I to get over the solid satisfaction that first job gave me of having money that I had earned myself jingling in my pockets. For the first time in my life I could make just as big a fool of myself with money as I liked. I certainly did. I never bought a useful thing, or saved a dollar.

After this defiance of my New England forebears, I went peacefully. Father and Tante drove up in a brand-new Maxwell car and took me home. It was September, and I was again a schoolboy.

The summer after the summer in Maine, I put in working for another railroad—this one the B & M, which was building what's called a Hump Yard beyond the North Station in Boston. That my health broke down, working in an open cut twenty feet deep in compacted sewerage, through 120° summer temperatures, was no more than an incident. The doctors decided it was all my tonsils' fault and when they took these out they considered their job finished. Unfortunately for me, they had inadvertently done something irreparable to my left eardrum. How they got to *that*, doing a tonsillectomy, I'll never know, but forty-five years later it is still ringing—although I've long since ceased to be more than occasionally conscious of it.

This was the summer that led into Hotchkiss School—I was barely on my feet again in time to show up—so that by the time I got there I had acquired my own kind of precocious sophistication. But I was still unprepared for what awaited me in Lakeville.

I felt that I had seen all sorts of people and things in my time but nothing that remotely resembled, in pretentious silliness, the students amongst whom I now found myself. Their plus fours and three-button herringbone jackets made me giggle. Moreover, they were schoolboys and, by God, I was a man who had earned his own living. Even the professors seemed silly to me, with their heavy-handed schoolboy jokes and their interminably slow instruction.

Hotchkiss's opinion of me was no better. I was a scarecrow dressed in outgrown ready mades, if not hand-me-downs. Also, I was clearly of the lower classes, because I was a scholarship boy, and, worse, "from the village."

So I said to hell with them all and let it go at that. If the snobs of Hotchkiss had their own arrogance, I had mine. For seven months of a winter that set records in New England for snow and ice and subzero temperatures, I lived on it. It wasn't a bad diet, and I grew to be very fond of the sunsets over the snowy Berkshire hills. At twilight there is great peace in them.

The Hotchkiss I am talking about was the pre-World War I edition, under a pompous headmaster who was known to us boys as "The King." Under successive administrations, I am told that its manners have improved. The school I knew, however, was the one in which new boys were forced to walk with one elbow touching the side-rails that ran the length of interminable corridors. It was the Hotchkiss in which upperclassmen disciplined lower by bringing them to trial for offenses against The Code, and administered punishment to those found guilty by making them run the gauntlet, naked and prickly with goose flesh after a cold shower, their executioners whipping them with knotted towels. It was a Hotchkiss costumed—uniformed, rather—by the New Haven tailors who came each fall and spring to set up shop in Lakeville. One earned one's H for success in Competitive Dressing.

It was a Hotchkiss, in short, whose whole emphasis was on conformity—and as already a burgeoning nonconformist, I can't recall a single happy hour in class or out; nor did I make a single friend.

But when spring came at last, and being alive was tolerable again, I did get myself involved in one lark that almost changed several people's lives. This began with the discovery by my classmates that I had access on weekends to the family car. It was parked in the barn on Tante's farm, only three miles away. So I was approached. Would I join in a conspiracy to pinch the car and drive three classmates twenty-five miles to Millbrook, for the daring purpose of calling on some young ladies in Miss Bennett's Junior College there? This *did* appeal to me. It involved breaking so many rules they could hardly be inventoried. It meant automatic dismissal to be caught outside the township without authority. I had neither permission to abduct the family car nor a license to drive it. So I said, "Sure!"

En route to the forbidden land, other obstacles emerged. The young ladies at Miss Bennett's, it was known, were allowed to receive only callers whose names were on written lists approved by their parents. Only two of the four of us were on anybody's list, but we had an inventory of eligibles to impersonate. After much conferring, it was decided that I might pass for somebody named McKeever who was on the list of a girl named Joan Bennett. Joan was a roommate of one of the other boys' girls. No one knew her personally—or that she was destined to become a famous movie star—but her roommate had said she was quick on the trigger. We broke up the conference and proceeded.

We arrived at Miss Bennett's, which has an imposing three-story stone-and-shingle main building, set in wide and sweeping tree-shaded lawns. All at first went well. Even the two who did know girls there gave fictitious names. This was the only thing that saved them in the end, because things did not go well for long.

While the girls were being sent for, we were seated in a parlor giving onto a second-story porch overlooking the lawn. The first two girls to come running in reacted like seasoned conspirators and hastened to embrace the boys who were supposed to be their cousins. The schoolmistress, hanging around to be sure that everything was on the up-and-up, was reassured. A third girl came, took the wink, and behaved all right.

All were now present but Joan. The schoolmistress had just

turned to leave us alone at last when we heard Joan's merry voice outside—"Johnny McKeever, Johnny McKeever, how in the world did you get here?"—and in she came, freezing in her tracks, her mouth dropping open at the sight of four young strangers, none of them Johnny McKeever. In vain did her room-mate wigwag and wink. Joan was still under full sail, and the first words that came to her—and because I had stepped forward she said them, loudly and clearly, directly at me—were, "But you're *not* Johnny McKeever!"

What happened next was unrehearsed. As the dragon turned to re-enter the room, all four of us males left by the only available exit—the French doors opening onto the porch. And the porch we left with leaps worthy of paratroopers, up and over the wooden railing and down fifteen feet to the turf below. The last that Bennett's saw of us was our backs, streaking around the end of the building toward the parked car.

We did the twenty-five miles back to Salisbury in thirty minutes flat, got the boiling car stowed in Tante's stable, and scattered back over the hills for the school grounds. We beat the roll that was called by half an hour. It had taken the scandalized Miss Bennett some time to organize her inquiry-by-telephone— she had a score of boys' schools to cover; there are that many within an hour's drive in the Berkshire hills.

Years later, one of Joan's famous sisters, Barbara, became a good friend of mine; but I never forgave Joan herself for muffing her lines that memorable afternoon.

After the Millbrook episode, my classmates and I might well have made peace. But it was too late; graduation was almost upon us.

v · Happy Time

For me, the summer of 1918 hung motionless in time, suspended between Hotchkiss School shutting down in May and Yale University reopening as a military establishment in September. I was seventeen, but so grown up now that I had to carry my birth certificate around with me to prove I wasn't a draft dodger. The family didn't know what to do with me, and I didn't either.

Then came a note from Cousin Alida asking if I would like

to spend the summer with the Temple Emmets at Stony Brook. Cousin Alida was Mrs. C-for-Christopher Temple Emmet. She had had seven or eight children and was still having them, and they all lived, with Cousin Temple himself, in a big rambling white clapboard house overlooking the Sound from the Long Island side.

I don't think that the Emmets were (or are) really cousins. I think we thought of each other as relatives because Alida and my mother had been close friends all their lives. Maybe there *is* some connection, way back; all the aunts and uncles who could set me straight are gone. But cousins or no cousins, I came to love them dearly.

The Emmets are an enormous clan, and almost all of them have that elusive and indefinable quality known as charm. And Alida was a Chanler, and all the Chanlers are supposed to be mad, in a happy kind of way. To remind you of it there was always Cousin John, who once went too far and was locked up for it. He's the one who sent the famous telegram from an insane asylum, on the occasion of his brother's divorce, which read, "Who's loony now?" It was to Brother Robert, who, when divorced by a famous singer named Lina Cavalieri, had had to mortgage his property for two hundred thousand dollars to meet the costs. The time was December of 1911. Brother John, who spelled his last name Chaloner, had been declared insane in New York but sane in Virginia.

Cousin Temple was tall, erect, and very good looking, and shy and gentle, with a musical speaking voice. Until he met Alida, he had studied forestry and hoped to spend his life in any wilderness that had trees in it. But Alida put a stop to all that. She said, "I'm going to have twelve children and I'm certainly not going to do all that way out in the woods." So she brought Temple down to Stony Brook and built a squash court on the place so that he could exercise and keep in shape, and she went to work to get her project under way. By 1917 there were Libba, Christopher T., Jr., Margaret, Hester, Winty, and Willy (these were twins, around ten), and one or two babies—I can't quite remember. The littlest ones were always considered Temple's personal property. He liked all children, but he loved little-bitty ones best, and since Alida always provided him with another as soon as one had begun to grow, he led a very happy life.

It was always rather a mystery where all the money came from that supported this almost enormous establishment—for most of the children had governesses or nurses of their own, of various nationalities, and it took a fair number of servants just to take care of, feed, and wait on the governesses and nurses alone. As I understood it, imperfectly I'm sure, there were assorted trust funds somewhere, mostly on the Chanler side. I have an idea there were some Astors among Alida's forebears. One of the original John Jacob (The Great) Astor's granddaughters was named Alida; another married into the Chanler family.

Anyway, one of the nice things about these trust funds was that they were not the stodgy reliable old things that sent dividends every month. Like their beneficiaries, they had temperament, too. One year they'd be feeling high, sending everyone to Europe and buying new Rollses. Then, all of a sudden, they'd start sulking, and there wouldn't be enough money to pay the servants, who were by then much too busy staving off creditors to quit.

Part of the Emmet charm was the way they handled these vagaries of fortune. They were totally unaffected by affluence or penury. In this, they were assisted by a wholly natural and spontaneous unworldliness and a kind of cosmic vagueness.

The first happy thing that happened to me when I went to live with them resulted from this fact. It was my discovery that I was not the oaf around the house that my engineering-minded father considered me. I was a genuine genius. This was first revealed when I happened upon a group of master and servants trying to decide what to do about an electric sconce that wouldn't light. I think they'd gotten down to arguing whether it was a mechanic or an electrician they should send for. After only the briefest of studies, I stepped forward. I screwed down a bulb and the thing burst into brilliance.

That evening I was the talk of the household. When I next repaired the table buzzer that took signals from the dining room to the kitchen, everyone was so proud of me I was fit to burst.

Believe me, I take no liberty with these stories. That summer the financial wind was blowing the wrong way, and three limousines, two of them imported, had been put on blocks to be replaced by Model T Fords, owner (instead of chauffeur) driven. Cousin Christopher, then eighteen, was the first to master these fascinating gadgets, and one day he drove me all the way across the Island to Forest Hills to watch a tennis match. Not far along on the return journey we blew a tire. Down went one side of the rear end and, bumping along on its rim, the whole car began to shake violently. But, to my amazement, Christopher, who was driving, hardly slowed down.

"Stop," I screamed, "stop and fix it."

Christopher thought about this advice for a few minutes but shook his head. "I wouldn't have the least idea what to do about it if I did," he replied, "and, besides, these aren't expensive, you know."

A mile or two more of this and, of course, the second rear tire went. This stabilized matters for a while, but the vibrations finally became too much for our forward end, and, one by one, the tires there went, too. We did the last five or ten miles, many of them in low gear, on rims; the radiator was in a fine, furious boil upon our arrival.

I was really shaken, psychologically as well as physically, for every engineer's instinct in me was violated. But Christopher alighted nonchalantly, smiled vaguely at the poor Model T, patted the cowling, and ventured, "If it was a horse, we'd have to shoot it, wouldn't we?"

When Cousin Temple proved to be no more than gently amused by our misadventure, I knew that I was in a new world.

My father was the kind of motorist who considers a half-empty gas tank a sign of negligence.

Many and wonderful were the results of Emmet vagueness. That year we still had our house on East Seventy-first Street in New York, left put up for the summer, as usual, with its furniture under dust covers, its family portraits mercifully hidden under cheesecloth. But since I had a key to it, it was natural that I should offer its use to the cousins with whom I was living. Two of the older girls put up there one night, chaperoned by a very strict Fräulein. They had all attended some concert and, characteristically, missed the last train back.

Surely nothing would have come of this if Fräulein hadn't been so busy getting the girls together and out of the house—after making the bed and tidying up my father's room, where they'd slept—that it hadn't occurred to her to check the little dressing room off the bath. On his next trip to town, my father did the checking for her. He turned up with one pair of panties, female, and some stockings.

I should have felt very pleased that this was put down to an indiscretion of mine except for the fact that when I had the hell bawled out of me for it, I hadn't the least idea what my father was talking about. It was a long time before I could put two and seven together and come up with the real story of what had happened.

What made such a truly deep impression on me at Stony Brook was not the eccentricity, but the truly genuine normality of a family life that I had never known. All of the Emmets loved each other, and because I was one of them now, they loved me. They were thoughtful of and interested in and amused by each other, endlessly. And they had a deep and effortless—"culture" is the only word you can use.

Over the years, a succession of governesses (and a season or two in Europe for this one or that) had made linguists of them all. Almost every member of the household spoke French and German, and their English had a music I didn't know my own language could make. The grand piano in one corner of the enormous living room was something one sat down at to amuse oneself by playing, anything from Czechoslovakian folk tunes to Mendelssohn. For those who couldn't play, there was a pianola attachment with a wonderful collections of rolls that I got to know almost by heart. And there was also a huge phonograph, an early Victor with an enormous horn suspended above it, whose records included not only the classics, but wonderful things like John McCormack doing Kipling's "The Hanging of Danny Deever" and all Harry Lauder's early records.

I suppose there were movies in town and other entertainment en masse available on Long Island, but we never went to any. The evenings I remember began with Cousin Temple reading Dickens or Scott aloud to Winty and Willy. We older children could listen, and usually did. Then someone would play a piece he liked, or we'd all just sit around amusing ourselves with conversation, laughing at the things that had happened that day or getting into some violently serious argument over whether there ever could be a better tennis player than Tilden; or we would talk sadly about the horrible war that was going on abroad. The Emmets were very sensitive to suffering.

Christopher was always going to or coming from some place, so Marga and Hester and I—who were within a year or two of each other's age—were a threesome. We spent most of our days down on the shore, at the foot of a cliff below the house where there was a place to bathe and miles and miles of shallow water to wade in and explore for crabs and jellyfish and things like that.

Libba, who was a year or two older than we were, was the orchid in the family. I have not wavered in my belief that she was the most beautiful human being I've ever seen in any country, on or off any stage. She was tall and fair and graceful, with features that were just enough off the classic Greek to give them a character and a distinction that were unique. And she had enormous eyes, the irises of which were true violet. The young figure that accompanied these graces was as perfect, although she was physically on the frail side. Libba must never have been very strong, for I remember her as often so pale as to seem unreal. But the paleness itself had a quality. Her skin seemed to give forth a delicate blue light, as if it were made of translucent alabaster. She did not live long after these years, but died when she was in her twenties, of what strange malady I do not know.

In 1917, however, the pallor I have described was no more than a premonition. Libba was as healthy and happy as any of us. It was only her extraordinary beauty that set her apart. One of the ways it accomplished this was to surround her constantly with so many awe-struck young males that you had, in effect, to keep pushing them apart to get near enough to Libba to have a word with her. When she was nineteen, any adult male who came under the spell seemed to have no choice but to drop all his other affairs and make up some excuse to move into the vicinity of Stony Brook, just to hang around. Since the Emmets were such extraordinarily polite people, no one seemed to have any idea of how to go about sorting them out and keeping them in hand.

Libba herself was as unaffected and vague about all this violent buzzing about her as you would expect of an Emmet. As Nordic blonde women sometimes are, I think she was physically immature for her age. All these men paying her so much attention bewildered her.

For those who fell seriously in love with her, Libba was an unsatisfyingly ill wind—but one that was finally to blow an adventure of some substance my way. It was because of Libba that I almost—though not quite—became a pilot in the Royal Flying Corps.

This was about August. Halfway down the island toward New York, His Majesty's airmen had taken over a field at Garden City, equipped it with Camels and Avros and staffed it with combat aces. I think this was some kind of a war-effort advertising stunt, or a place they could rest their fighter pilots from combat fatigue, or both. Anyway, Garden City was not so far from Stony Brook that word of Libba's existence didn't get from the one place to the other; and presently we had half the Royal Air Force buzzing our front lawn, and their most glamorous characters dropping in for tea every afternoon. An old hand at annoying my sisters' beaux, I gave Libba what help I could in distracting them—for I was wholly fascinated.

To get rid of me, it was inevitable that a Group Captain should invite me for a ride. I didn't know, and wouldn't have cared if I had known, that the invitation was wholly malicious—a chance to scare me (in my role of little brother) so thoroughly that I should never come back for more. So the next thing I knew I was knocking on the door of their Officers' Mess one afternoon to take the Group Captain up on the offer. He must have rubbed his hands with glee. The whole squadron broke out to dress me in overalls and helmet and goggles, hoist me up, and wedge me into the tiny front cockpit of a two-seater—and off we went on my first flight.

I was told later that we climbed to ten thousand feet—I remember that. Then all of a sudden the plane went over on its back, began diving, twisting, twirling, looping, spinning, skidding, plummeting, and turning itself inside out. I had been too excited to eat, thank God! But vomiting seemed to be the only unpleasant sensation I was spared. When we dropped the last three thousand feet, sideslipped over the tops of the trees by the field, and bumped to a stop, I was so totally disassembled that I wouldn't have known my own name if I had been asked. And when we taxied up to the hangar, there they all were, waiting appreciatively to enjoy my misery.

The trouble with their joke was that when they got me out of their contraption, I was too speechless to say anything that would give them a laugh. The world was still spinning, and I had to hold on to the plane with one hand just to stand up. The only thing I could think of to say, when I did get my breath, was, "Gee, but I loved that."

Inasmuch as the next thing I did was to fall flat on my face and pass out, this speech of mine was considered as not less than "a bit of all right." Very strange people, these British. From being the butt of their joke, I was now the hero. Presently I was the center of an admiring group in a bar, where I was being revived with Pink Lady cocktails—the first hard liquor of any kind I had more than tasted.

After two Pink Ladies, I decided that the opportunity was far-and-away too good to waste. Clearly I must have talent for this kind of thing. The devil with the United States Army and the Students' Army Training Corps, which I was supposed to join within the month! I would leave home and enlist in the Royal Flying Corps right now. And I so announced.

Thus it was that before I was poured back into one of Cousin Temple's remaining Model T's, and sent on my way home, I had, tucked in my pocket, a bona fide letter of introduction and recommendation from Group Captain So-and-So to Air Marshal Hoare (I'll never forget *that* name) in Montreal. I had not even had to lie to get it, for, unlike the United States Army, the Royal Flying Corps had no prejudice at all against seventeen-year-olds.

So tremendous was this whole experience that I actually survived the impact of four Pink Ladies without becoming intoxicated, and, driving carefully the whole way home—lest anything happen to a body that now belonged to the British war effort—I plotted the movements that would take me from Long Island, U.S.A., to Montreal, Canada, without falling afoul of my family. I knew I had no chance of getting *their* sanction.

The summer at Stony Brook had done its job; I felt that I was again master of my own destiny. I was rapidly freeing myself from three depressed years of teenhood, during which I had allowed myself to be battered about by family decisions on what was best for me. I had recaptured my confidence with new dimensions, dimensions that the gentleness and true sweetness of the Emmet family had given me, without design or effort.

It was wholly natural that in this process I had fallen in love—with Marga, whom I thought of as my cousin. Marga was not nearly so beautiful as Libba. She had delicately russet-colored hair and, in place of Libba's alabaster, barely discernible freckles. But of all the musical Emmets, she had the most musical voice, and a little laugh that was truly like the rippling of a mountain brook. She was more graceful than the others, and loved to run like a puppy or a small child just for the fun of running.

Marga was also considered—affectionately—quite mad. This was mostly because of the sailor. This was the sailor she talked to in a tree at night, the sailor in the old apple tree at the far end of the lawn that nobody else but Marga could see or hear. Marga had known the sailor for a long time, and often talked with him for hours, although he was not always there when she went to seek him. Since this relationship had gone on for years, it is a true measure of the Temple Emmets that Marga could bring up the sailor in conversation naturally, and discuss him seriously, without any of the family getting particularly excited about it.

The Emmets were quite capable of accepting the sailor without other evidence than Marga's, and I've often wondered if Joan the Maid would ever have become a heroine of France if *her* family had reacted as casually to *her* vision. In due time, I understand, the sailor faded away for good; but in 1917 he was very real, and Marga often discussed me with him.

Marga and I fell in love without any effort at all—or any embarrassment. And our feeling for each other was accepted by the rest as casually as they accepted the sailor. We were neither thrown together—our families would have very much approved —nor pulled apart. The sweetest memories of all my life, I think, are long afternoons on a little ledge we made our own, halfway up the cliff above the Sound, with the wind below us ruffling the shallow water and making the reeds whisper and yet no breath of it touching us.

The memories are of Marga half lying there, innocently, her

brown eyes aglow with pleasure, singing to me. She sang strange little songs in many languages, for she was the most gifted linguist of them all and knew Polish and Czechoslovakian songs that someone had taught her. Her voice was very young and child-like. These were hours when there was neither past nor future and the moment was wholly sufficient unto itself.

I don't know what became of this love which Marga and I just had between us and never got around to talking about or planning for. Marga herself was neither shy nor forward, but I had some kind of prohibition on me. I knew, at one and the same time, but had no idea how I knew, that Marga was at once the most desirable thing in the world and the most unalterably forbidden. I knew, with an infinite sadness that made me cry when I was alone, that she was what I wanted more than any-thing else in the world—but would never have.

The full knowledge of this, without any reasonable explanation that I could give myself, came to me about the time of my ad-venture with the R.F.C. In the end, I fled Stony Brook as much to escape an intolerable emotion as to seek adventure in the air. Never at any time did this make sense to me; it was simply an adolescent compulsion, and I was as inarticulate with myself as with Marga. It was a long time before I saw her again, and by then it was all gone.

The running away to Montreal was not to work out either—but the end of that was Booth Tarkington comedy.

The first part of my carefully studied plan was a working alliance with an Emmet cousin by the name of Chanler Chap-man (his schoolmates called him Charlie Chaplin, of course). Chanler was no older than I, but he had one formidable advan-tage: his older brother, Victor, had successfully enlisted in the famous Lafayette Escadrille, which flew with the French. And Victor had subsequently been killed in action, the first American pilot the Escadrille lost. Chanler had dedicated himself to emu-lating his brother; and for obvious reasons his family had dedi-cated themselves to frustrating him.

The gist of our plan was that we separate, to avoid suspicion, and meet again in New York, where we would entrain for Canada. We had train schedules and money saved from our allowances for one-way tickets. The meeting place we chose in New York was a saloon on West Forty-second Street. This was a bit of bravado, for neither of us had been in a saloon before, anywhere; but a forbidden spot seemed appropriate.

We got that far all right, but, huddled conspiratorially over our beers, Chanler wanted to know where my luggage was. I didn't have any.

"You'll just have to get some," Chanler persisted. "They'll pick you up on a train if you haven't luggage." And neither of us had draft cards.

I suspect that what had Chanler confused was some conversation he had overheard about having to have luggage to get into a hotel; but I was convinced that he must know what he was talking about.

The upshot was that I made an attempt to sneak into 167 East Seventy-first Street, now reinhabited by my father and his new wife, to purloin a bag. And of course by that time I was, as my sisters would have put it, "stinking of beer." So I got myself nabbed and sat down to a "now-what-is-all-this-about" talk.

Next day I learned that Chanler had gotten himself caught as easily as I.

Life is hard on young adventurers.

VI · It Takes All Kinds of Freshmen

"I was educated at Yale University, graduating in 1921 with a B.S. in Mining Engineering." What a multitude of blunders, confusions, emotional mishmash, and misinformation, half baked and quarter absorbed, that simple statement recalls!

In the first place, the assumption that there is "a Yale education" in my background is itself false. "A Yale education" implies four years' exposure to the conservative influences of a great American university—and I had no such thing.

What I attended was Sheffield Scientific School, then (if no longer) a semiautonomous institution. Legally, it was Yale University's, but, spiritually, it had its own customs and culture. When I was there, the University had already begun the process by which it has since assimilated Sheff into the undergraduate school with the institution of a common freshman year, the lengthening of the undergraduate course from three years to four, the breaking up of the whole body of undergraduates into English-type "Houses"—Davenport, Stillman, and the like.

My class—1921—was Sheff's last three-year job. But I wasn't there even the three specified years. For the first half of what should have been my freshman year, there was no Yale University. It had been taken over by the U. S. Army as a branch of World War I's Student Army Training Corps organization. I served in the uniform of the S.A.T.C. from September until the end of 1918, living in dormitories converted into barracks, being drilled on the old Yale campus and marched to and from classrooms.

I wasn't even an honest-to-God soldier in the S.A.T.C. I was only seventeen and had to serve as a tolerated volunteer, without serial number, pay, or veteran's rights.

When the S.A.T.C. was demobilized, I came back to New Haven for a freshman year that lasted only five months—after which I was suddenly an upperclassman!

So even if Yale had been a settled university when I attended, I wouldn't have been there long enough to acquire much patina. But in their first postwar years, no American universities could have been described as "settled." Practically the entire student body at New Haven was just out of uniform; a sizable percentage were only yesterday returned from overseas. They were more like soldiers on furlough than young students. Campus life seemed silly to most. The taboos of tradition had lost their hold. Anything went, and the atmosphere was of anarchy, not ivy.

The professors were back and classes were held. As an engineering student, I took a minimum of forty-five hours a week of them, and one term as many as fifty-seven. (Children seem to feel put upon if asked to take more than fifteen nowadays, despite the current superstition that scholastic standards are higher than in my day.) But I cannot recall my studies ever seriously distracting me from the pursuit of undergraduate happiness.

Perhaps that was my temperament and a by-product of my being—what is it called?—"a quick study"? I have always had, and still have, a flair for rapid comprehension, a knack of photographing impressions, from reading rapidly, listening or looking intensely. The negative so exposed is anything but permanent, and since I have all my life been impatient and anxious to get on to the next subject or experience, real scholarship is beyond me. But I have all my life irritated those whose knowledge is more soundly founded, by being able to get the gist, and just enough chapter and verse of their specialty to create a false impression of real understanding. In my student days, this made it reasonably easy for me to get good-enough marks to permit me to go on about my true business, which was trying to finish growing up.

Anyway, looking back, I have few regrets that I did not absorb more of the science I was exposed to, or, rather, absorb it more permanently. As far as I can see, everything I was taught at Yale University in 1920 and '21—everything about the nature of the real world we live in—has since been proven to be fraudulent. We were taught that sixty-four was the irreducible number of elements composing matter. It has since turned out that there is only one "matter," different structures of which are called atoms.

The biggest scientific joke in history—I chuckled at it, along with my learned professors—was the medieval search for a lodestone that would turn lead into gold. But now, I understand, the medievalists were right all the time. It *can* be done, by rearranging atoms. Even a straight line ceased to be the shortest distance between two points, circa Einstein!

So perhaps my instinct not to take the scientific knowledge

of my time too seriously was sound after all. Actually, I had begun to be a skeptic along those lines when I was in my early teens. When the family moved into our first house with electric lights in it, I was fascinated. But no books my scientifically oriented father could find for me could explain it beyond the empirical observation that it just was. One could arrange for its creation, and handle it, after a fashion, after it was created— but what was it to begin with? No books could tell me then, and I soon concluded that the attempts to define it were sheer bluffs.

Today I see no reason for disbelieving the logic that if everything about the nature of matter that I was so seriously taught in 1920 has, by only 1960, been found to be unsound, then it is entirely possible that what my children are learning from the pundits in the sixties will be bosh to the pundits of the eighties.

Remembering such thoughts I can only sigh. I present them here as apologia for the frivolousness of my approach to formal education. But only for some aspects, because in the real world of 1918, when I reached New Haven, I was the eagerest of eager beavers, anxious only to be of service to my fellow countrymen. For there was a war on—and I was about to be in it.

So next comes the story of the Student Army Training Corps' battalions at Yale University—or, rather, of my small and insignificant experience therein.

In the fall of 1918, as I've mentioned, I was still seventeen. But I was already a good six feet two inches tall, skinny, long-haired (for want of the patience to stop regularly at a barber's), and shambling.

Everyone was keyed high in 1918, with a world to be saved for democracy. But nobody had to whoop it up for me. I had just been through a humiliating year when I'd had to carry my birth certificate with me to explain to authorities why my ungainly length wasn't already in uniform. I was exhilarated beyond any measure when I finally did make it. There had been a terrifying hour when I almost didn't. A nasty little doctor with spectacles

and a bald head had marked out the shape of my heart with red
crayon on my hairless chest. That is the way they did it in those
days. "Too big," he said. "Have you ever had rheumatic fever?"
But I got so furious that I must have frightened him, and he
passed me.

Twenty-some years and one World War later, the doctors used
X rays instead of red crayon. At that time they found something
they did not like about my lung, but I talked them out of that
one, too. Lord knows why I did, after my experience with my
first war, which for me meant only sixteen hours a day of closely
supervised study—not in a war, but in freshman calculus,
mechanical drawing, and physics.

A favorite story of my disenchantment with soldiering used to
be of how I made sergeant my first day in World War I, corporal
the next, and private on the third and thereafter.

I have to set this scene by explaining that the first thing that
the Army took over at Yale was its campus, which was a smallish
area of discouraged grass completely surrounded by a wooden
fence—the one on which captains of Yale football teams get
their pictures taken—and solid ranks of six-story dormitories.
Inside this arena, the company to which I was assigned was
drawn up in line, and a shiny young man barked at us sharply,
"All those with previous military experience, one step forward."

So, of course, out I stepped—for had I not once, at the age
of twelve, worn the proud uniform of a chichi children's drill
corps, called the Knickerbocker Grays? I gave the Lieutenant
my name.

"All right, Private Ingersoll," said the Lieutenant, "you are
now Sergeant Ingersoll. Take over the company."

I should now explain that the company I took over had had
the benefit of no more than ten days' instruction in the rudiments
of close-order drill. But the men *were* organized into squads and
had a speaking acquaintance with simple commands like "Forward March," "Squads Right" and "Squads Left," and "Halt."
So did I—barely.

In the close confines of the historic Yale campus I got my one hundred and ninety men first in a column of squads and then into what is known as a "company front." But by then they were unhappily facing, and bearing down in full stride on, the good old Yale fence. In panic I measured the rapidly dwindling distance that separated the two lines, the moving and the unmovable. And then and there my tongue refused to function. As in a nightmare, I was speechless.

With jubilant smiles, and miraculously in step for the first time in their military careers, my one hundred and ninety soldiers stepped briskly into the fence as if it were not there, tumbled over it, crossed the pavement, and piled up flat against the dormitory, still going through burlesqued motions as of marching.

"Sergeant Ingersoll," bellowed the Lieutenant, "you are now Corporal Ingersoll. Company halt, fall out, and reform."

The day after the debacle on the campus, I was given command of the first squad—squads being numbered in order of descending altitude and I being the tallest man in the company. That was the beginning of my new trouble.

When another and more competent sergeant marched us from the campus to the mess hall, half a mile away, it was my squad that stepped out first. On the return trip, logically, my squad became the last.

On my first predawn sally from breakfast as a corporal, I soon became aware that one member in the rear of my squad was making rough weather of it. He had, in brief, one hell of a hangover. No one, least of all I, could blame him for the effect breakfast had had on his condition. Starched French toast with Karo had been the *pièce de résistance*. So it was no surprise to me when, en route back to the barracks, the poor man began to vomit. But it did tend to spread out the neat and orderly symmetry of my squad. The men to either side of the poor fellow fell rapidly away to the right and left, and my front rank bolted on the heels of the squad ahead of us.

At this precise moment, whom should we come past but the

Colonel of the entire regiment, standing alone in the dawn light, counting heads. He was a wizened little cavalry officer brought out of retirement to train us, but, like the well-known howling ape, he could generate sound out of all proportion to his size.

Old soldier that he was, the Colonel handled the matter of my squad's dishevelment through channels. He bellowed for the Captain, and the Captain bellowed for the Lieutenant, and the Lieutenant bellowed for the Sergeant, and the Sergeant made a private out of me.

That was the last authority I was trusted with in World War I. By the end of the war, we had seven former corporals in our squad.

All of our strictly military training at New Haven in World War I seemed also to border on farce. The command consisted of half a dozen two-hundred-men batteries of embryo artillerymen, a company of premedical students, and my own of would-be engineers. There seemed to be something about the lot of us that made us fundamentally incapable of pleasing officers charged with beating sword carriers out of plowboys.

These officers had, for the most part, been drawn from junior classes at West Point, and, to a man, they felt demeaned by their assignment. There was no glory to be won drilling Yale students, and the best we could provide was an outlet for their frustrated aggressions. Thus it was a standing order that if one private offended, his whole company was punished, and if one company failed to pass inspection, the whole battalion would get it in the neck.

Our working day lasted from five in the morning until ten at night, with a single half-hour break from formations after retreat. The only time left to take away from us was our Saturday afternoons and Sundays. So three Saturdays out of four the whole battalion spent the afternoon waiting for the last sloppy one of us to get his dirty little face shaved right or his buttons sewed on properly or his spiral puttees wrapped according to regulations.

The whole business was a nightmare from which there was no awakening. The food we were given to eat seemed so inedible and inadequate that only the ingenuity of Connecticut Yankees, I think, kept us alive. It was not the Army, but enterprising local citizenry that converted trucks into pie wagons and stationed them outside the classrooms. Tumbling down the steps from the halls of learning, with the sergeants barking at us to line up fast, we could still exchange quarters for pies and stuff them into ourselves on the dead run. In four morning breaks—if you had a dollar to begin with—you could manage to get four whole pies into yourself. After this, the noon meal could function as a savory.

Militarily, the whole business was nonsense. The artillery never fired a cannon nor the infantry a rifle. Educationally, it seemed to be the government's serious intention to cram three years of science into our heads in twelve months, after which we would be turned loose as qualified engineer officers. Fortunately for all concerned, the war had only three more months of life in it, and the effectiveness of a scientific education so acquired was never tested.

Emotionally, all I can recall was my first experience with naked, savage hatred—not of the enemy across the sea, but of the shavetails and their sergeants here at home. Their discipline had that quality of irrational unfairness that made their delight in causing men to be miserable seem sadistic.

Nor could it have been all in my imagination, for there were horror stories among us. One boy had actually fought in France as a soldier in the Foreign Legion. When America entered the war, he had come back patriotically to join his own army only by some fluke to find himself in our midst. For two weeks he took all the bunkum and the barking philosophically. Then one afternoon of boredom was one too many and he simply dropped out of the ranks and went to a movie. There the M.P.'s picked him up, and, believe it or not, he was court-martialed, found guilty of being A.W.O.L., and sent to Leavenworth as a prisoner.

It was twenty-four years after World War I before I found

myself in another American army. This one bore so little resemblance to the first that I found it difficult to understand how the same civilization could have brought forth two such dissimilar establishments. With all the waste and confusion that is inherent in any organization put together for the purpose of mass butchery, the American Army of World War II was so much more reasonable than its predecessor that it is difficult to compare them.

To me, the end of the S.A.T.C. was as enraging as the beginning. With the blowing of factory whistles for the Armistice, it should have been over, but, instead, on Armistice Day itself, with the city going mad all around us, we were actually locked in our barracks, and only turned out the next day, for a victory parade. Four more hours of marching with rifle and pack through the still-hysterical crowds of civilians! And then we were marched back to the campus without once being allowed to break ranks.

For six more weeks it went on, but after that it really was over.

It was when I took up life again as a genuine Yale freshman that I acquired my first ally. His imposing name was Louis Faugeres Bishop. He had been a friend of my childhood in New York, and I had met him again the summer before at Stony Brook, when he, too, had been bound for Yale's S.A.T.C. Impulsively, we had agreed to room together "after the war," and in January made good our pact by moving together into a big sunshiny room in a dormitory called Van Sheff.

Getting our first look at each other since Stony Brook, I doubt if either of us was reassured. The affable Park Avenue heart specialist of today was then a rather scrawny, habitually frowning young man, absent-minded enough to have been a professor. And Lord knows what he thought of me, decked out again in my old store-bought civilian clothes, now outgrown; they had shocked the Hotchkiss boys even when they fitted me. But at least we had shared the nightmare of the S.A.T.C., and *that* was over.

But whatever Bish and I thought of each other was soon to

prove less absorbing than what the upperclassmen of our time thought of both of us. This was when each of us in turn was rejected by the fraternities that dominated our undergraduate life.

Things are different now, but in those days Sheff undergraduates slept and ate in houses maintained by the brotherhoods. If none of these select institutions wanted you, you had to fend for yourself—find your own rooms, make your own new friends, eat on the town. And the Social-with-a-capital-S lines were drawn hard and fast.

The ritual of sorting the goats from the sheep was known as Calling Week. For five or six days of a certain week that was set apart each spring, freshmen received formal invitations to pay formal calls on specific fraternities between fixed hours. The first day of the week, an eligible might receive engraved invitations from all. The next day he would be dropped off the invitation lists of fraternities that had lost interest in him. If he was still in the running, say for Colony, they would ask him back every night of the week, on the last of which they would make him a member.

Delta Psi had been my father's society. And Bishop's father had been a member of St. Elmo's, so that he, too, was a "heritage," meaning that he, too, might expect to be elected automatically, as a matter of course.

But it was a tense week for everybody, with each of us up against a situation that was new to us, portentous and, in some mysterious way, promising either better or worse fortune in the future. Also, it was a matter beyond our power to influence. Clearly it was impossible to make an impression on these awesome upperclassmen on whom we waited. They had not been awesome yesterday. But now they were. And if my memory is correct, our hosts were as ill at ease as we, all dressed up and on their party manners. I remember, on one call, stupidly spilling something and having several seniors rush to help me mop it up. They made me giggle.

Anyway, nobody ever told Bish and me how the two fraternities involved came to their separate decisions to turn us down.

We'd each of us been asked five nights in a row but not the pay-off night. That night, we had sat together in our room, like spinsters waiting for a telephone call that we hoped against hope would come but knew in our hearts would not. For we must have cast the die ourselves, months earlier—serious-minded little Bishop by leaving his classmates behind him at St. Paul's (he had skipped the sixth form), and I by bringing my own private claque of detractors with me from Hotchkiss.

Within twenty-four hours after the choosing, we were both sure that our worst fears had been realized. Everything was changed. The carefree group of boys who had come out of the Army to enjoy each other's company at their parents' expense had been sliced in two as with a knife. The frosting was now on the other side from us. Those of us who were denied it now looked at each other with new eyes, seeking new alliances within what was now our "class," in the sociological sense. It was with great sadness that we concluded that our lives had been permanently blighted.

But still, it was spring.

In New Haven in 1919, spring really did burst out all over—in the most memorable and bloody town-and-gown riot of modern time. It lasted for three days and three nights, several innocent bystanders were killed, and several score were hospitalized. And, except for the casualties, everybody concerned had a marvelous time—which is why I felt so abused at not having been in it.

The reason I was not on hand for this affair was that I was ignominiously hospitalized at the time, from infectious boils, acquired as a wrestler. So I missed all the fun.

The whole thing began simply enough. There was a parade. It was to celebrate the return of the veterans, and its route of march led past the Yale campus. The City of New Haven put it on. All veterans were urged to march, and an invitation was duly printed in the *Yale Daily News*.

But the undergraduate reaction to this courtesy was a resounding horselaugh. Student veterans had done their marching; the American Legion found few recruits among them.

When the day for the parade came, however, some embryo stuffed shirts got out their old S.A.T.C. uniforms, put them on, and joined the marchers.

The parade itself had bands, of course, and when it came abreast of the campus, these bands drew heads to windows. Soon these heads had many a coarse comment to make on the military below. This might have been enough to start trouble, but when the students in the windows saw some of their own classmates in the ranks, their joy and derision knew no bounds. Those who were hapless enough to boast an S.A.T.C. ancestry, everyone felt, had it coming to them.

Maybe a few things did get thrown out the windows. Anyway, enough happened to encourage the newspapers in New Haven to print a scathing editorial denouncing the bad manners of the clearly unpatriotic Yale student body.

And that still might have been all right if the editorial writer hadn't gotten carried away and included in his dithyramb a suggestion to the citizens of New Haven to *do something about it.* They did.

Some veterans' organization announced that it would hold a mass meeting of protest on the New Haven Commons the following noon—and the newspaper had to go and box *that* on the front page. It was an invitation to every hoodlum within trolley trip of New Haven to come and join the fun. Several thousand showed up. On this assembled multitude, some rabble rousers went to work, and within the hour—and a convenient lunch hour it was, too—the ranks had swelled to ten thousand strong. Finally someone yelled, "What are we waiting for? Let's go get 'em"—and the show was on.

New Haven's ancient green abuts the old Yale campus, the strong high gates of which could be hastily closed. But the Yale campus is only a small part of the University, which spreads out over a square mile or two to the west and north. Breaking against

the fortress that the campus now became, the mob split and began overflowing adjacent streets, smashing windows and overturn-
ing cars as it went. And also, as a matter of course, beating the hell
out of anyone who looked like a student of Yale University. The
hallmark of a student then being his hatlessness, anyone with
the bad luck to be uncovered got beaten up. Since the seniors in
New Haven's high schools were also against headgear, an appalling number of them were casualties.

I don't think anyone knew exactly how the riot came to acquire
such momentum that it took several days and nights to stop it. I
put it down to the counterattacks that soon began developing.
Students on the Academic campus, who'd been locked in, managed to get out, through the windows. And Sheff Town couldn't
be locked up. Within hours, counter gangs had been recruited and
were at work. On their side, the Townies kept bringing up rein-
forcements from mill towns like Branford and Bridgeport. These
always were tough places. On both sides, all sense of proportion
was soon lost in the melee of flying fists—and on and on it went.

A wonderful example of a typical misfortune was what happened to a boy named Roland M. ("Poly") Hooker. (He was
later to become one of my best friends, but I didn't know him
then.) Hooker had been off on a binge the day the shooting
began and returned to town, the second night, in a beautiful
robin's-egg-blue Pierce Arrow touring car with the top down,
accompanied by three other undergraduates and two young ladies.
They had driven innocently down Chapel Street and turned into
an alleyway by the old Hyperion Theater, which led to the
garage where Hooker stabled his car. A small splinter group of
fifty or sixty Townies saw him making the turn and followed such
conspicuous evidence of student affluence down the alley.

In those days, it was not characteristic of Roland M. Hooker
to return from a binge stone sober. And indeed he was not when,
coming to rest in the garage, he looked up to find himself surrounded by grim countenances. He was six feet three inches tall
and had bright red hair. Clearly he was not going to sit there

and do nothing. But beside him sat a smoother and much more self-possessed classmate, who stood up and took charge before Hooker could move. This one asked the ringleader what it was all about, and was told. Thereupon he launched into a brilliant and reasonable defense of his own and his fellows' credentials.

"I myself," he said, "served two years at sea on a submarine chaser. And this gentleman here," he said pointing to Hooker, "was twice decorated for bravery in action. We're on your side, brother veterans."

A breath of approval ruffled the upturned faces of his audience. He had just about won the day when some dim and confused version of what was going on finally made its way into Hooker's head. Wriggling from behind the wheel, he stood up and pushed his persuasive advocate out of the way.

"These bastards," he announced in a loud, clear, and very deep bass voice, "killed my father and my mother and now the sons of bitches want to kill me."

He was never able to recollect what made him say that, because when he came to, he was in the New Haven General Hospital with his jaw broken in four places. The odd rib or two and collarbone, he didn't count. It was the broken jaw, which interrupted his career as a tankard man, that bothered him.

Meanwhile, an even grimmer little playlet was being enacted below the windows of Bishop's and my room in Van Sheff. A mob of several hundred, roaming up Temple Street, had seen the lights in the Van Sheff windows just across the yard. Only a six-foot-high fence of wooden palings separated them. The fence went down before the first charge, and the horde swarmed shouting over the flat turf beyond. They bore down on an areaway that is the back entrance to the Van Sheff dormitory, and from which a stairway ascended to the room in which Bishop and I lived. This is, of course, a secondhand description, but it came from eyewitnesses.

Twenty or thirty feet from the areaway, the mob halted to reform, with insults being shouted back and forth between the front rank of the attack force and the dormitory's garrison. In the dormitory rooms, they were breaking off bedposts to use as weapons.

At this juncture, a young man who lived across the hall from Bishop and me—and who actually had put in some months in action abroad—could brook no more of it. From his bureau drawer he took his service forty-five automatic, put a clip in it, and went down to meet the mob alone. No one saw him go, but his appearance, floodlit by the overhead light in the areaway, standing alone in his shirt sleeves facing several hundred roaring mobsters, is sharply remembered by the men in the windows.

And then at one and the same moment both the watchers in the windows and the mobsters opposite him saw the gun in his hand. There was sudden and almost complete silence, which the former Argonne doughboy broke by saying, in a low but distinct voice, "After I count three, I am going to begin shooting."

Then he did count three and did begin shooting. He dropped three men in succession—in an arc reading from left to right. By this time, since he had shot slowly, there were no more targets; never had a mob been seen to disperse faster.

Within seconds, Horatio's horrified classmates were upon him from the rear. He was disarmed, undressed, and shoved under a cold shower while a hasty council of war decided where to hide his gun. It was put as far up a chimney as the smallest available student could be wedged. When the police came, a dozen guns were confiscated, but none of them was a forty-five. And, happily, none of the victims was dead.

These stories are typical of the three days and nights of the Great Riot of 1919. The New Haven police had never at any time even approached the ability to calm things down. It was strongly suspected by the students that their hearts were not in it, as long as more students than Townies were being beaten up. Hostility between the New Haven Police Force and Yale students has over a century of tradition behind it.

The Governor of Connecticut was working on getting the militia out when the Fire Department took over. It was the Fire Department that put out the fire. Strategically stationed pumpers with high-pressure hoses cooled out first one group and then another, and the violence sputtered and went out.

I have not studied the history of undergraduate riots, but I suspect that spring is the natural season for them. It is also, and eminently, the season for girls. And in New Haven in my day girls meant Chapel Street and Chapel Street meant girls.

To residents, of course, Chapel Street is simply the east-west artery that divides uptown from down—and also the City from the University. South of Chapel lies the business district of New Haven, its warehouses, and, finally, the railway station; to the north there are the post office and civic buildings, the better residential districts, and, just west of them, Yale University. On Chapel itself, facing the Green and the University, there are, in succession, the biggest department store in town (Malley's) and the Taft Hotel, which is often thought of as an outpost of Broadway because it stands next door to the Shubert Theater. At the Shubert, they try out so many Broadway productions that the lobby of the Taft always seems to bulge with actors and actresses, harassed producers, press agents, and distraught playwrights—when they aren't crowded into oblivion by a football crowd bound for the Yale Bowl.

To the men who play football in the bowl, Chapel Street is a much simpler thing; it's the place where you pick up girls. That is, it was for a long succession of generations, including my own. Maybe it isn't any more. Maybe the Cocktail Lounge, which didn't exist in my day, has taken over. But Chapel Street was a trysting place as far back as my father's time. In those college scrapbooks of Father's there are sketches showing Chapel Street girls in exaggerated bustles carrying parasols and being bowed to by scheming young men in tight-fitting pants. Their bowler hats were always respectfully tipped.

Father, of course, never explained such phenomena to me, ever. All the sex education I got from him was brief and to the point. When he was driving with me back to college after some vacation or other—in my eighteenth or nineteenth year—he said suddenly, apropos only of a long silence: "Be careful when you get to New Haven, boy; don't ever run around with a mill girl." I was too startled to ask what memories prompted the remark. I never did find out. My father's icy reserve when the subject of sex entered the conversation was always too formidable for me to crack.

His repertoire, however, did include one risqué joke, which he would retell from time to time under very special circumstances. It was about a tiny little man who was annoying a great big buxom woman by following her about. When she could stand it no longer, she called a policeman and had the little man arrested. He'd been tagging after her all day long. When they got to the police station, the big desk sergeant looked down at the little man and shook his head.

"Whyever would you be doing such a thing, annoying this nice lady that's done you no harm?"

"Meaning no offense, sir," said the little man, "I was just charging my battery."

A faint blush always illumined my father's flowing and snowy-white mustache when he told this tale, which must have been right on the button when the Leyden jar was first invented.

When you're eighteen and it's spring, no one's batteries need charging. And the young ladies who strolled on Chapel Street in my day were not yet sophisticated enough to distinguish between students who were members of fraternities and outcasts like Bish and me. They were not ladies of light virtue—really. Or let's put it, rather, that they had their self-respect. Most had jobs, many of them in Malley's, so that when they came off work they had simply to tarry on Chapel Street a while in case something should turn up. Their curious pride was that they went out only with Yale students. To socialize with their brothers' friends, they considered beneath them—little snobs that they were rapidly becoming. And, of course, for self-protection they always hunted in pairs and knew well how to administer the brisk brush-off. The crusher, in 1919, was "Oh, be your age!"

If nothing promising turned up on Chapel Street, young ladies on the prowl would then proceed to a moving-picture house a few blocks away, just off Church, the street that intersects Chapel to make New Haven's Broadway and Forty-second Street. There, the male signal that interest had been aroused was given by moving over and sitting directly behind the young ladies, who, of course, had already given *their* signal by sitting in front of two unoccupied seats.

In the moving-picture house, further approach was not oral. It was distinctly bad form to speak first. You simply reached a leg out under the seat in front of you, and knew where you stood by how hard it was kicked. This was called "Playing Footy" and sometimes went on for a long while.

It was during this phase that conversation could begin—but not between boys and girls. The girls discussed the boys, each speaking only to the other, and the boys discussed the girls, in clearly audible tones, so that the frank and scathing quality of the sarcasm could be appreciated. When, as—and if—wits were seen to match, the bargain was made.

What happened next depended, of course, upon whether the particular students involved were in funds that evening. The girls understood this. For them it was a game of chance whether the payoff was a single beer, which had to be nursed all evening, or a taxi down to Savin Rock for a shore dinner—and it was etiquette for them not to wheedle. They were really very nice girls.

At Savin Rock, if they made it, the party found a pleasant provincial amusement park, complete with a roller coaster and a tunnel of love. Going there had charm, but what gave it thrill was the common knowledge that it bordered a certain row of dingy clapboard houses. These had once been mansions but were now available to the public as houses of assignation. They had names like Jimmy's and Joe's, and they were all alike. In the downstairs parlor, there was a bar where cheap liquor was sold for a dollar

a one-ounce whisky glass—and you could sit around there getting
up your courage to rent one of the rooms upstairs.

The acquiescence of a Chapel Street girl to be taken to Savin
Rock most definitely did not include a commitment to proceed
with you to Jimmy's or Joe's. That part was optional—or, rather,
it was up to you to make it seem inviting enough for a girl to risk
cross-questioning when she got home. For home she would go—
eventually—but if Savin Rock included Jimmy's, she knew darned
well she'd be late, and maybe smelling of whisky.

So the usual process of initiation into manhood for the Yale
freshman in those days involved a series of forays over a period
of weeks, each one getting closer and closer to Jimmy's or Joe's,
and, finally, in a turbulence of conflicting emotions, "making the
grade," as it was put.

The actual act itself was never very pretty. It had usually
taken too much whisky to get up nerve enough to be there at
all, for everybody was very shy about everything. It was, for instance, against the rules to leave a light turned on. A girl might
go to bed with you, but she'd sooner die than let you see her in
her slip.

Also, everybody was very ill at ease afterward and usually
remorseful. These were not love affairs. They were part of the
ritual process of growing up; and they were rites conducted by
amateurs. The most vivid memory I have of my own rite is the
number of cigarettes my young lady had to light and smoke down
to a stub that burned her before she would condescend to begin.

These mores were so rigidly enforced that few had the courage
to stand up against them. There was no quicker way to real
ostracization than to defy them. One result was that those who
were too timid, or lived by other and stronger taboos, had often
to resort to falsehood. The gentle art of boasting about doing
something you hadn't was widely practiced among males of my
acquaintance. In the end, however, it was the girls themselves
who outdid us all.

How this happened is a story of true poetic justice. You must
understand that in these first postwar years, the forces of Virtue

marched as gallantly as the forces of Vice. Postwar Chapel Street had no sooner revived its traditional role in undergraduate life than the mothers of New Haven organized their own counter-offensive. These were years when the Noble Experiment of Prohibition was in the making.

In New Haven there came into being a Society for the Prevention of Student Vice, put together and manned by middle-aged female vigilantes. Their number swelled until they were able to force a grudging co-operation from the Police Department. There were sermons from the pulpits and there was propaganda in the press. And it was a great lark to us students—till one day all the humor went out of it in a real-live police raid complete with patrol wagons.

What seemed strange at first was that the raid was staged not at Jimmy's or Joe's, but on Chapel Street itself, from which several dozen hapless girls were hustled into paddy wagons and packed off to police stations.

Presently the plot revealed itself. It was the plan of the Society for the Prevention of Student Vice to give the girls the verbal works and thereby extract from them the names of the students with whom they'd been to Jimmy's and Joe's—on promise of immunity. These names were then to be turned over to the University authorities with the request that the boys be expelled as a threat to the virtue of New Haven womanhood.

From one end of Ac to the other end of Sheff, there was panic; that's the only word for it.

But everything came out all right after all. With the wit that only the hunted have, the young ladies in the calaboose came up with the only solution that could have saved the day. Instead of clamming up, they sang; and of what did they sing? They sang the names of famous drips who were well known not to have gone out with anybody. They gave, to a dozen innocents, reputations no wastrel would have had the time to acquire. And darned if a couple of these didn't get expelled, because, as one of our heroines said of her tormentors, "Gee whiz, those dames believed anything!"

VII · Sophistication at Home

The war had so thoroughly telescoped my career as an under-graduate at New Haven that after only a few months as a fresh-man, I came back to New Haven with a junior's rights and privileges.

Privilege number one was to choose a career to study for. I had done no thinking about my life or what I might care to do with it since that summer in Maine. I had been too busy trying to adjust myself to what life was doing to me. But after my freshman year was over, I got up courage to tell Father that, much as I enjoyed his supporting me in New Haven, I still couldn't see being the kind of engineer whose bridges were ordered from a catalogue. This led to my being sent down to New York to talk with a cousin-called-uncle who was a mining engineer. It was Uncle Jack who sold me on mining—by warning that I would have to expect to live my life in faraway places. I was for that.

Actually, Uncle Jack's endorsement of the Yale School of Mines must have cost his conscience something. There were then only two really accredited courses in mining engineering in the United States, one given by the Colorado School of Mines and the other by Columbia University. But a man named John Hays Hammond, who had made a lot of money mining something, had given Yale several millions of dollars to set up a shop in competition with the established schools. So heeled, the University had built a new metallurgical laboratory out on Hillhouse Avenue and hired a faculty. Since word of these facilities had hardly startled the mining world, I found that I had signed up for a class that was outnumbered by its professors, something like eight to five. We were a very select little group, and remained so.

By a happy turn of fate, the next two years of my life were to be spent with an equally select group of friends and house-mates, none of whom Bishop and I had ever laid eyes on before meeting them at 360 Temple Street.

Having been turned down by the fraternities, Bishop and I should have been shopping all over New Haven to find rooms we could rent. But in acquiring land for future expansion, the University had come into possession of a two-story clapboard house that had been a landmark in New Haven for generations. It is a landmark still, although not in New Haven. Not many years after we lived there, the late Henry Ford bought the building itself, had it taken apart, transported to Dearborn, and reassembled there. It is a feature of his museum of early Americana. Its claim to fame is that it is the house in which Noah Webster wrote his dictionary.

In 1919, the University made this memorable structure available to students who had no fraternity to harbor them, and Bish and I landed there. Since its location, at the corner of Grove and Temple Streets, was directly across from St. Elmo's and Vernon Hall, it was practically a fraternity house itself—and it was the work of a single term to turn it into one. We called it the 360 Club, and we had our own little gold emblems manufactured for us. A bas-relief of a small pocket flask was our fraternity pin. It symbolized our coming into existence with the Volstead Act. It was to acquire considerable local fame before we were through with it.

The first fame of 360 was as a gambling joint. It got off to a flying start the afternoon I first walked into the big bay-windowed room on the Grove Street side where Bishop and I were to spend the next two years. Its only furniture then was a battered old table, but around this were grouped half a dozen trespassers sitting on empty boxes, engaged in an informal game of Red Dog. Giving them my credentials as their host, I pulled up a box myself, and the next thing I knew I had a couple of months' allowance in a pot that was growing to formidable dimensions. It was all very exhilarating, a far cry from the sober scholastic existence Bishop and I had lived in Van Sheff. I could see that life was going to be different as a junior.

Red Dog is a table-stakes game, and soon the fifty dollars that I contributed was but a modest fraction of the pot. The boy across bet twenty dollars on a card, and lost; there was a sudden awe-struck hush when I heard myself calmly saying, "Bet the pot itself." The card was turned up—and I had won something like four or five hundred dollars. In the rustle of impressed comment that followed, somebody behind my left shoulder sputtered, "Gee, but he must be loaded"—and not for moments did I realize that he meant me.

After that, the word was out that if you wanted a game played for high stakes, drop in at 360 Temple. One curious result of this was that we who lived in 360, from being a heterogeneous group of nobodies, suddenly found ourselves somebodies. The whole structure of our relations with the rest of the undergraduates was built around gambling. As members of the unwashed, outside the fraternity walls, we hardly rated a "Hi" when passing one of the elite on the sidewalk. But now it was the elite who sought us out and to whom we gave, or denied, *our* hospitality. Gamblers have always had a nebulous kind of acceptance by the upper classes.

In addition, gambling was, for me, a solid source of income. My frugal father was thoroughly retired by now and living on the income from his life savings. He had little money to spare for me after paying my tuition. I forget exactly how much spending money I got, but it was somewhere around twenty-five dollars a month, on which it was not possible to live the life of a Young Gentleman. I kept my bills paid to the tune of "two no trump, doubled" and "two will get you eight the hard way."

It should by now begin to be apparent to the reader that the first postwar years in New Haven lacked that kind of morality taught in Yale's Divinity School. They did, and gambling, which was by no means confined to 360 Temple Street, was only one symptom. Cribbing in classrooms and on examinations passed the phase of undergraduate sanction. It was presently to become a fine art.

We had one boy in our tiny mining and metallurgical group whom I will now name Pullian. He was an engaging little fellow whom everybody liked, but, unfortunately, at the time he seemed a little short on both money and academic knowledge. What was done about his shortage of funds I'll come to. The immediate story concerns Pullian's congenital inability to understand the principles and practices of a course known as Thermodynamics.

Thermodynamics was a real stinker, and it was required in order to get an engineering degree. Pullian's friends speedily agreed that something would have to be done about it. You could write his papers for him at night and you could slip him notes in the classroom; you could encourage him to sit behind someone who knew the right answers. But you also just knew that you couldn't get enough into his head to get him through the two-hour final exam.

Bear in mind—as evidence of the moral atmosphere—that Joe Pullian was not a famous football player. Neither was he the sweetheart of Sigma Chi, although he did belong to one of the fraternities. He was just a nice little guy who was having a really hard time getting by.

When the final exam finally came, it was agreed that there were only two men in the class who might save him, and that the only way even they could do it would be by taking the whole exam for him. One of the two men tapped was the only *magna cum laude* student in our group. He was an Irish boy from New Haven itself, gentle, sensitive, and shy; he was anything but one of the boys. Moreover, the character that was one day to bring him to the top of his profession, and make his integrity a byword, was already apparent; he was the soul of honesty. And he was deeply religious to boot. But he was enlisted—and saw nothing wrong in the role he was to play!

Neither did I, when I was the other man elected to save Pullian's bacon. Unlike Bill Cummings, I was not on the team for my prowess with mathematical theory. I was there because I was thought to be ingenious. They put it up to me to find a way by which Cummings could take the exam for Pullian. And this is how I did it.

The examination was to be held in a study hall several blocks from 360 Temple Street. Scouting the problem, I found that one window of its second-story classroom looked out on a lawn separating the study hall from the nearest building. With a painstaking attention to detail worthy of a Brink robbery, I figured that the questions in the examination could be scrunched into a spitball, thrown out the window, and caught by a confederate. Several candidates for catcher were considered, and a man on the track team was chosen, a sprinter. The time it took him to run from the study hall to below the bay window of my room was clocked. Arrived there, the runner had then only to throw the spitball up to a second catcher in the bay window. Once he had the questions, all Cummings would have to do would be to work out the answers, which could then be run back and thrown up to Pullian through the open window in the examination room.

So far so good—but as soon as I put the timetable down on paper, I immediately saw the flaw. It was a two-hour examination, known to be so tough that even many "A" students failed to finish it. And Pullian was a slow laborious writer. How could we make up the time he would lose copying off the answers we gave him? The cribbing staff would have to complete the paper in less than half the alloted time—and not even our genius Cummings was up to that.

So I had to invent some more machinery. In front of the bay window, I installed two card tables, adjoining. At one of these tables Cummings was to sit, and I would sit at the other. I was to get the examination paper first, race down it and snip off, with a pair of shears, the questions I thought I could handle. The tough ones I was to slide across to Cummings.

Then we drew on our reserves for two quick-minded, competent scholars and sat them, one each on the remaining sides of the tables, with open logarithm books to look up our tables for us. After a dry run, we were pretty sure we could now handle any two-hour job the faculty could throw at us in not over twenty-five minutes.

And that's the way it worked, without a single hitch. Pullian succeeded in misreading just enough of our answers to provide the necessary margin of mistakes, without which he might have been suspected.

The *magna cum laude* scholar, as I've suggested, now holds a position of international importance in the scientific world. The last time I saw him was a year or two ago, and that meeting comes back to me now, because one of the things he happened to mention was that he'd run into Pullian recently, at some learned conclave he was conducting.

"Good God," I said, "what was Pullian doing *there?*"

"Oh," said Cummings, "he's the president of one of the big oil companies now."

I admit that when the subject of cribbing first came into general circulation in bull sessions, it got a considerable nudge from my New England conscience. The subject made me very unhappy for a while and I had no choice but to ask myself where I stood. The answer that I gave myself, at nineteen, was that it was foolish and shortsighted to crib for myself—and a waste of Father's money—but that there could be no harm in helping others. They would surely suffer by not having put themselves to the discipline of mastering their subjects—but that was their business, not mine. I had a very positive feeling, then, that I was not my brother's keeper. The trait I most admired in human beings was tolerance, and morality preached was anathema to me.

In defense of Yale's postwar class of 1921, I would like to put down that wine, women, gambling, and a license to crib were their only vices. Unfortunately, this is not entirely true. There was a distinct tendency to condone stealing too, if the theft were committed gaily and in a good cause. I said I would tell how Pullian's tendency to run short of money was corrected. He got to be such a pet of all of us that whenever he needed a new tie or shirt—or possibly an overcoat; that might be harder—somebody stole it for him from one of the stores that served the campus. Pullian didn't steal for himself but I think one boy who stole for him stole for himself as well. (What happened to him in later life? At the peak of his career he was the managing editor of a metropolitan newspaper. May still be.)

All this talk about morality has carried me a little way afield, and a bit ahead of my story. None of the principals in the above tale were housemates at 360, whose occupants had other eccentricities. Most charming—and most enraging—were Poly Hooker's, that same Poly Hooker who had had his jaw broken in the Great Riot of the year before.

When we came together at 360, Hooker was our only celebrity.

He was best known for that robin's-egg-blue Pierce Arrow touring car, which was now parked daily outside our front door as if to advertise that there was something special about us. That was one of the years when the Pierce Arrow had its headlights welded to the top of its far-flung fenders. Poly's was one of those models. It seemed to us to be one hundred sixty-seven feet long. There were twelve of us in the house at 360, but the Pierce Arrow could, and did on occasion, hold us all. No one else in the entire University owned such a car.

Poly, however, did not need the Pierce Arrow to advertise himself. He had a deep booming bass voice, which emerged from a face that looked like the profile on Cannon Mountain. Above that stood the brightest and most profuse crop of carrot-red hair.

Poly's mother, who had white hair and was almost as big as he, used to come to visit him sometimes. She was the widow of a former mayor of Hartford, Connecticut. Hooker was also a descendant of some of the founders of that city. As the then last of his line, he was never denied anything that his mother's money could buy.

Those days, as I have suggested, the thing that Hooker was not denying himself most of was whisky, and one of the minor miracles of the class of '21 was how Hooker managed to stay in it and still consume something close to a quart a day.

A probable explanation for Poly's ability to get at least passing grades was the additionally curious fact that he was far and away the best-educated boy in school. Before he'd taken up liquor, Poly had devoted a lonely childhood—he had been tutored rather than schooled—to books. In the old family mansion in Hartford, he had operated in the only room I've ever seen that had all four walls, from floor to very high ceiling, solidly stacked with books. There were no windows in the room at all, just the door through which you went in and came out. Poly told me, and not as a boast, that he had read every book in the room.

The nature of this enormous thing that was Hooker was so gentle and unassuming and generous that before he graduated, a sizable segment of the University lived on his handouts, drank his liquor, borrowed his car, and otherwise exploited him. Exploit is too strong a word. Villagers who drink at the only free-flowing spring in town don't consider that they are exploiting it.

The whole of Hooker's life since he left college has been fabulous, and he has been both richer than his family ever was and much poorer. Latterly, he has reverted to his scholarship days (which preceded his college education), and is a historian and genealogist, living in a cheerful bungalow in Miami and drinking mostly beer.

No one else in 360 Temple could hold a candle to Hooker as a character—not even Parsons, who had amnesia after his second small drink of whisky and used to come back after one of his spells in all sorts of curious conditions, once stark naked except for his overcoat and shoes. It was great fun trying to guess what in the devil had happened to Parsons when he came back after a blackout. He would rediscover himself under unusual circumstances, too. Once, he heard himself taking up the call "Is there a doctor in the house who can help this poor devil?" only to have the man next to him (in a football stadium) shout, "Sit down, you damn fool, it's you I'm calling one for."

Almost everyone in 360 had an eccentricity of some kind; one of mine was playing the most morbid music I could find on a new phonograph. I played each record over and over again until it drove everyone but Bishop bats. During these spells I would lapse into a kind of ecstasy of melancholia. The sadder life got to seem, the more I loved it, and I always came to from these binges relaxed and refreshed.

The reason my record-playing never bothered Bishop, I think, was that he never heard it. About junior year, Bishop's anxiety lest he flunk out as a premedical student became so intense that he was as if in a permanent trance himself.

Once, to keep awake for an all-night wrestle with Organic Chemistry—his personal Thermodynamics course—Bishop got undressed and went downstairs to take a cold shower. Still muttering formulas to himself, he turned left instead of right and found himself—it was about 10:00 P.M.—out the front door and stark naked on Temple Street. A passing classmate noticed this and said, "My God, Bishop, what are you doing out here?" This challenge so startled Faugeres that, after looking down and becoming for the first time aware of his nakedness, instead of turning back into the house, he took off down the street. Thinking he'd gone suddenly mad, his classmate took off after him. And away they went, at a bolt gallop, with Bishop picking up pursuers, as shouts and footsteps spread the alarm. At least Bishop had the presence of mind, once under way, to keep making right turns at successive corners and so was successful, after circumnavigating the entire Sheff campus, in popping back into 360.

Alerted as to what was going on, residents of 360 Temple were waiting to whisk the hare out of sight and to divert the hounds. It is a measure of the affection and loyalty that 360 had for Bishop that four men, shoulder to shoulder, barred the way to what was by now a sizable pack clamoring to follow the naked sprinter into the house to find out what it was all about.

"It's none of your damn business," pronounced our spokesman. "In *this* house we take the air as we please."

VIII · Educationally Speaking

In New Haven, as an undergraduate, I had turned my ostracization by the fraternities into a happy thing by the device of inventing the 360 Club. In New York, which was only an hour and a half away, I had a happy time, too. It was my first as what Harry Luce's magazine writers call a Socialite. My vacations and most weekends, in 1920 and 1921, I spent in New York gathering no moss whatever.

At Hotchkiss I might have been an oaf, in New Haven no

fraternity would have me, but there was nothing whatever the matter with my social standing in New York. As a properly registered member in the aristocracy, as both an Ingersoll and a McAllister I was in demand far beyond my due in that Society which spells itself with a capital S.

Where was I registered and what was the Society I am speaking of now? It was not the Society of my childhood and Mother's time. It was the post-World War I era, when "new" fortunes were again challenging the old order, waging war with more and more lavish coming-out parties for their daughters.

The new titans' wives were anxious for the presence at their affairs of members of the older families. Registry as a bona fide member of the in group was, first of all, the family's listing in the social register. Cleveland Amory names 1925 as the height of this curious organ's power of discrimination. But listing here was taken for granted. There were other more secret lists that it was vital to be on. These were lists that were sold, like social introductions to a European court, lists on which ambitious hostesses could rely when they made up *their* lists of the eligibles to invite to their daughters' dances, to ask to dinner. One of the lists supported a formidable old lady who lived next door to us on Seventy-first Street and who was always complaining that the noise from our piano came through the walls and disturbed her. Presumably she required silence for her meditations on who was really who.

I have no idea how it works now, and suspect that it was all rather more formal then, although Society seemed to my elders horribly casual after World War I. The chaperones required to police my sisters were gone, and so were the formal dinners with ten or twelve courses. Boys no longer invariably wore white ties and tails, as had been required only a few years earlier—and the next thing you knew there would not even be starch in their shirt fronts! Moreover, nice girls now used rouge—almost all of them —and some even smoked (although not, of course, in public).

But Coming Out—the phrase "making a debut" was considered

affected and possibly *nouveau riche*—was still a very formal and individual affair. Girls were not herded together in cotillions then, to make cut-rate appearances; if you couldn't afford to bring your daughter out with a party of her own, then it was up to one of your richer relatives to rally round and give her the party. And the party had to be a climactic effort, like the wedding of a peasant's eldest daughter, a public demonstration of the best show you could afford, even if you had to borrow the money to do it.

Five thousand dollars was considered a fair ante, and five thousand 1919 dollars was a lot of money. But five thousand dollars wasn't anything like a ceiling. Among the debutante parties that I can remember, the all-time All-American was in a copper magnate's mansion on upper Fifth Avenue. It sported a curving grand staircase leading from the baronial entrance hall to the second floor, and this was banked solidly, from top to bottom, with crisply fresh orchids. Instead of two orchestras—which were S.O.P. for a party in a hotel—there were three.

It was the invariable custom at a debutante's party to serve a simple breakfast, usually of scrambled eggs and tiny sausages, around 2:00 A.M. At even the most elaborate parties in the old Ritz, these were informal buffets, with the young men standing in line with their own plate in one hand and their girl's in another. At my party-to-end-all-parties, everyone was seated, grouped at tables of four. To serve each table there were *two* butlers in livery! Moreover, there were two champagne buckets, with a quart of champagne in each of them, at each and every table.

That copper magnate wasn't fooling around, nor were his young male guests under any illusion about why, for not only was he barely out of the copper mines himself, but he also had the homeliest daughter that anyone had tried to foist off on us for a long time.

The young men on the stag line were every bit as snotty as that then—and probably still are, for young men in those circumstances are hothouse fruit and spoil rapidly.

The real wonder of it is that any of us ever recovered, for, every year, hundreds of thousands of dollars were spent putting on shows clearly aimed at entrapping us. We had no reason to believe we weren't the most important things in God's creation— the "we" referring to the young men on the list the Lady Next Door prepared.

In a good season at Christmas holiday time, I never had less than half a dozen invitations for every single weekday night, Saturday not excepted. Manners having gone down the World War I drain, none of these required acknowledgment, despite their carefully engraved R.S.V.P.'s. Nor did it ever occur to anyone to thank a host and hostess for an affair that might have set them back a life's savings.

A lot of parties you never went to; you just knew they'd be deadly. "Deadly" would have been my sisters' word. We boys used words that were much sharper and less respectful, but I can't remember them. Those parties that looked promising, one might drop in on, condescending to give a half hour of one's valuable time.

Even at that social altitude, not many parents lived in houses as big as the copper magnate's, and most of the best parties were at the old Ritz, on Forty-sixth and Madison. The Ritz was that wonderful old hotel—it wasn't so old then—made immortal by Ludwig Bemelmans, whose Hotel Splendide was really the Ritz. He was a captain there before he became an artist and writer. It had a real air about it, and there never has been a hotel so well designed, architecturally, for glamorous entertainment.

In the first place, downstairs there was the oval ballroom, ringed by tables raised a few feet from the floor so that you could look out over it. And right above was the grand ballroom, high-ceilinged, with long and sweeping drapes and crystal chandeliers. There the orchestras could play from balconies under which there were recesses where bars were set up and buffets laid out.

From one of these recesses, a private elevator led up to quarters which the host for the evening would take for the entertainment of selected guests. And the whole building seemed to be honeycombed with handsomely carpeted stairways on which you could sit out a dance with your girl. Your knees were in the necks of the couple on the stair tread below but that was okay.

Often in the Ritz there would be two rival shows on the same night, one in the oval room and one upstairs. But for the big bust, your host should have taken both.

Next to the Ritz came the Plaza—but one had to be very sure of one's self to put on a party in the Plaza. It was also available to "people from the West Side," with whom it was sudden death to be confused. The Ritz was most emphatically *not* available to the West Side. It was so popular it could afford not to be.

There were no other hotels that really counted.

The next step down—as seen from the stag line—was a party at the Colony Club. The Colony Club was, and still is, the female counterpart of the all-male Union Club. Its impressive building on Park Avenue and Sixty-second Street was only a generation old then. My mother had been one of its early members. The Colony Club was the place the rich relative usually chose when it was up to her to bring poor Mary out. It was impeccably correct, Socially, and it was also a lot cheaper. Clubs, like other co-operative enterprises, don't have to show profits.

An invitation to a debutante party at the Colony Club was fair warning that a poor relative was being put on the block; the music would be mediocre, the refreshments the same old thing, and the floor was sure to be uninvitingly ringed with elderly female relatives there to see the young people have a good time.

The Colony Club's were the kind of parties that your family was likely to insist that you attend, under orders to dance with the stellar attraction and be nice to her parents. At a party that was any kind of party at all, it would be impossible for you to get a dance with your hostess. The hallmark of her success would be that she could dance with no one for more than a few steps before being cut in on, for the stags had to outnumber the girls by at least four to one or any self-respecting male would walk out on the whole thing. Too much danger of getting stuck.

Each season, after you had been to a few dances only, if you were on the right list, you began to get invitations to dinners and private parties as well, also from people you had not known before. At these affairs, the males had only to outnumber the females by two to one.

Through all of this gay round I moved for a year or two as in a dream. Presumably the fortunes spent entertaining me were because I was an eligible suitor for the daughters. But I was no catch of any kind for anybody. I had, of course, neither money nor prospects, but that did not seem to matter. That was the crazy way it was, and the crazy competition that was New York Society post-World War I. But don't believe that I did not have a fine time enjoying the parties with my nights turned into days (which I spent sleeping, of course) one vacation after another.

Among the girls, I was known, and not always in the complimentary sense, as a "dancing fool." I did, indeed, in those days, "just love to dance," for the fun of it and even though "it really wasn't done." It was definitely gauche to appear to be enjoying yourself. The correct way to hold a girl was with one arm limp, looking down at her as if she were something slightly distasteful. The motion that accompanied this pose, if you had any aspirations to be chic, was a slow bored shuffle. But me, I grabbed them, and I danced with them, and *some* of them liked it.

The time I put in at parties in New York while I was an undergraduate at New Haven was the nearest I ever got to leading a social life.

Thinking back on those days, I can see that I had already begun my career as a young man with a foot in both camps. Three sixty Temple Street was an irreverent Bohemia. Its raucous crap games were a far cry from polite society among the well-heeled. Perhaps it was because I had such a good time with both that I was never after to be wholly content with either. The time was passing so pleasantly that I soon found my next revolt indefinitely postponed. Once again, my revolt was to have been against my family's gods—most particularly my father's personal deity, a career in engineering.

I had found no inspiration in the study of mining and metallurgy. Switching goals from my father's kind of engineering to my uncle's wasn't working. I knew in my heart that I was simply postponing an inevitable showdown between my father's creed and one that I felt, desperately, I must work out for myself to fit my own strange pattern. It was *words,* not figures, I had always felt, that would one day set me free.

That theme runs back into my earliest childhood. Like most boys, I had started a daily diary around the age of ten—but mine I kept, without missing a day, until I was a grown man. In addition, before I was even in my teens, there was the year I taught myself to use a typewriter by typing endless tales of adventure, which I made up as I went along. They were bloodcurdling Westerns mostly. But when I was the editor of the *Kirmayer Echo* at fourteen or fifteen, I turned it from disjointed paragraphs by semiliterate schoolboys into a journal principally devoted to publishing my own continued narratives of adventures overseas, fighting in armored cars with the Allies.

Meanwhile, my career as a writer was given an inadvertent boost by my father. He could hardly have been less interested than he was in literature as such. Engineering journals and an occasional biography of someone whom he admired made up his reading. But somewhere in his career as an engineer, he had picked up a conviction that became almost a crotchet with him. This was that all engineers suffered from their inability to express themselves with words, were unable to advance or define their projects before politicians or boards of corporations principally because they were inarticulate. To arm his son against such inadequacy, he did a really thoughtful job of encouraging me in thoughtful reading as well as writing. The device he used was ingenious.

I was to be paid—in true engineering fashion, at one cent a percentage point—for book reviews. The arrangement was a huge success. I not only read everything I could get my hands on, and with a new intensity, but I had thereafter to set myself down to tell my father what was in the book. I put this down to the fact that there was money in it, and money is as important to small boys as to grown males.

I do not belong to the school that believes that the distractions of the early twentieth century were vastly less than those of the Television Era. In my childhood, as I remember it, there seemed one hundred demands on every hour I had to spare. Every asphalt street beckoned me to roller skate on it; my gang's clubhouse meetings had homework for an eternal enemy. There were movies, soda shops, and an endless succession of passionate interests, all totally distracting—and there seemed to me to be just as much tut-tutting among my elders about how successfully we wasted our time as there is today about young television viewers. Two of my own sons, now at school, see no television at all. But they are still wonderfully ingenious about working up interests that have priority over homework. "Hacking" is their generic name for such activities.

All that is slightly aside, but it does remind me that by the time I found myself a freshman in New Haven, I must have written literally hundreds of thousands of words of my own composition. It is not particularly strange, then, that when I thought of wriggling out of the career that had been chosen for me, I dreamed of the written word as the solution.

As a freshman I had even received heady encouragement by having been given an A plus for a whole term's work in English composition after attending a single session. This is how it happened. During the first hour, the hour the class was organized, an ambitious young instructor announced that his objective would be to develop the individuality of each man's style. To give himself some idea of the material with which he had to work, he explained, he would like each of us to sit down that very night and dash off a short essay—no requirements as to subject, length, or organization.

Taking him happily at his word, I did indeed "dash off" two or three thousand words, on what was then uppermost in my mind—debutante dances in New York. And I turned it in that evening.

When I showed up in class next morning, the first thing I heard was my own name called. I thought I was going to get it in the neck for my frivolous theme, but when I went up to the professor's desk, my paper lay in front of him marked "A+."

"Ingersoll," he said to me, "you have a real feeling for satire. I don't want to spoil it with academic teaching. So, I tell you what I'll do: you stay away from classes in composition from now on and I'll give you an 'A+' for the year."

And he did!

The title of the piece that so overwhelmed this extraordinarily perceptive young man was "The Application of the Darwinian Theory to the Institution of the Stag Line." It was my belief that only the fittest could survive at a New York party. Unfortunately —I suppose life is like that—it was the last piece of satirical writing I ever did.

But everything else that happened to me as an undergraduate writer set me back. After the Darwinian Theory episode, the next thing I did was to look over the undergraduate publications to decide which one to conquer. The "Oldest College Daily" seemed to me pedestrian; the *Lit,* pretentious and affected. That left the humorous *Record,* but that didn't seem to me so very humorous, and I had no confidence that I was the man who could make it so.

At this juncture—and it seemed a happy omen—a group of Academic upperclassmen took it into their heads to start a new and livelier publication which would be devoted to fiction and light satire.

I tried fiction first, and after considerable effort produced a three-thousand-word short story which I modestly considered good. I took it around to the offices of the new group, confident that I would soon be one of them. A week later I got the piece back with a note saying that the editors just couldn't see the plot—only to pick up the next issue and find that the story I had submitted had been rewritten only slightly and published under the name of the editor who'd rejected the original.

Now you might have thought that in my undergraduate's code the normal reaction to this would have been a hasty interview and a punch in the nose. And probably it was. But I had been very strictly brought up to believe that the way a gentleman handled a cheat was to cut him dead. So, still under this influence, I wrote the incident off under the heading of experience. My hurt pride I salved by reminding myself that all undergraduate activity was childish anyway.

I may have henceforth cut him dead, but I never forgot the name of the young man who pinched my story. I marked him well—and only wish I could have bet on his subsequent career. It came out exactly as I might, even at nineteen, have been able to prophesy. He went to Hollywood, where he made himself a success as a motion-picture producer.

Disillusioned by underground plagiarism, my next step was to try to find a commercial outlet for my talent. But when the first six or seven stories I sent out came back with no more than the usual printed slips, I concluded sadly that it was into the mines for me after all.

Only one ray of sunshine relieved this dismal picture of the discouraged author. After the story of my success in English Composition got around, I was waited on by a succession of classmates asking assistance in their own English work. That was the time I had first to consider my own ethics in the matter of cribbing.

The answer I came up with was eventually to prove almost as profitable as Red Dog. I got so much business I had to standardize my rates, and put a few people on the waiting list. I charged fifteen dollars for an A, ten for a B, and five for a C; nothing whatever if the paper failed.

This new undertaking proved not only profitable, but great fun.

It gave me my first experience in what I might call creative editing. With a dozen or more clients on my hands, I had to study the style of each in order intelligently to imitate it, for clearly it was important that each man's work be consistent. I consider that I plied my crooked trade honorably; if I thought one of my clients no better than a C student, I never wrote him better than C themes, even though it cost me money to be so scrupulous. Maybe this is what eased my conscience—because I thought I had one.

Broadly speaking, this was to have been a chapter about the year I spent in New Haven as a junior. That should always be an undergraduate's happiest year, and so it was with me. I was adjusted at last to my environment, and the real world that waits beyond graduation was still far enough away to be unreal.

Out of all the months that make up any college year, those of spring should be the happiest. Mine in New Haven were, too. It was Nan who made them so—Nan Moran.

How the Moran part got in the picture I never knew, because you could have sworn that Nan was pure south Italian, with high color showing through her olive skin and jet-black eyes and very luxurious soft black hair. She was a very pretty young girl, almost beautiful, and I got to know her by taking a dare.

The dare was that I might think myself a lad at Savin Rock but would never have the nerve to pick up the one girl whose reputation was so torrid that even the fastest seniors were afraid to be seen with her.

Poor Nan! She had earned such notoriety, not by granting favors, but by withholding them. The true story of her young life—she was only eighteen or nineteen—was that during the war years she had had a serious beau with whom she'd been in love. He had gone the way of all undergraduates, the year before I met her, and Nan had kept her sadness to herself. She had made no more alliances. But hers was a dull life, lived with her working mother and two older brothers in a dreary section of New Haven. So she kept in touch with her old girl friends, and often went along with them for the early rounds of their evenings. She'd have a beer or two at the Hofbrau, or ride as far as the amusement-park part of Savin Rock—and then come back alone on the trolley. Since Nan's friends were of New Haven's fast set, the men whom she walked out on were, like as not, to report back to the campus that she hadn't. After all, they had their own reputations to look out for.

I am an authority on Nan Moran's life because for a long time after I took the dare and caught up with her alone in a movie one evening, she was my best friend in New Haven, male or female. The malicious magic that had fashioned her reputation as a *femme fatale* fascinated me then, and still fascinates me. It was my first lesson in being skeptical of anybody's reputation, whether evil or good. For Nan Moran was one of the nicest human beings I have known, and bore no resemblance to the verbal caricature I had been given of her. She had a warm and human kind of— gentility, I think the word should be—and much better manners than her detractors. She had natural taste, in her manners, in her reactions, and in her appreciations. It was not long before we left the world that had brought us together as far behind as we were able.

Most of the time Nan and I could manage to be together we spent in sunny fields, or the shade of some orchard far away from everything that was usual in both our lives. The happy circumstance that Poly Hooker was now my pal made all this possible. He had traded his big Pierce Arrow for a Stutz Bearcat, and I had first call on it when he wasn't using it himself. Nan and I did the whole north half of Connecticut, village by side road by village, before we were through with Hooker's generosity. And I will always owe him these hours.

At this point, I was about to be carried away by sentiment revived and to tell all kinds of things of which I am anything but sure; such as that Nan became the first real confidante I ever had and was my first true love. Stopping to take a long breath, I discard both concepts. We had a happy boy-and-girl relationship, Nan and I; we were even, for a short while, young lovers. But that's all I really remember.

It is an interesting study in the nature of memory, writing an autobiography. Whenever there were real emotions—whether of pain or pleasure—people and places come back to me, sharp and clear. So do things that at the time seemed to me humorous, or paradoxical, or ironic. The things that were monotonously dull, like the study of metallurgy, or simply pleasant, like my relationship with Nan, never really cut deeply.

I think of the years that I put in either simply enjoying myself or working intensely but moved by some motive that was not really my own as years in which I didn't live at all. And, conversely, there are the periods of tense feeling that may have lasted only months or weeks—or even moments. These seem years long in the experience of living.

I had a very wise man for a business partner once who felt the same way I do about these things. He used to measure the age of his friends with a calendar of his own. A bank president with whom he dealt, he considered as no more than sixteen real years old—"been so frightened all his life, it stunted his growth." My partner was in his sixties at the time; he modestly considered himself as approaching a thousand, measured by emotionally felt experience. I was still in my forties; he gave me the credit for being at least three hundred—but doubted if I would make the half-millennium mark. He felt that approaching middle-age I was already beginning to shy from violent emotional entanglements. To this man, it was a sign of old age to duck any emotion. He was, of course, an enormous egotist, and although, in his time, he has paid huge prices for his mistakes, he never considered any of them really expensive. He felt that he had lived so much longer by making them.

So judged, my relationship with Nan—which at the time seemed no mistake at all—was a sheer waste of our time, because neither of us fell deeply in love with the other. We just had a wonderful time and enjoyed every minute of it. And ended—both of us—by falling in love with other people, and wishing each other well.

Actually, the spring of my junior year at New Haven passed so rapidly that it seemed over before it was begun.

But there was one campus incident that also distinguished it from other springs, and this was an unpremeditated adventure in the field of academic controversy, and my first notoriety.

It was with the utmost innocence that I precipitated myself onto the front pages of the newspapers and the President of the University's carpet. The story of it is the story of my first crusade and includes my first tangling with Henry Robinson Luce, whose Vice-President and General Manager I was one day to become.

It all began when my roommate Bishop came back from one of his classes one evening in a lather. The class had been Biology, and its students had just got word that their professor's contract would not be renewed. This might have been routine except for the fact that the professor was young and extremely popular with his students, while the heads of the Biology Department were neither. And, in addition, they were of *German* extraction! Feelings stirred by a war to rid the world of German influence were still running high.

Another member of 360 was in the same Biology class as Bishop, a boy named Diefendorf, who was the son of a prominent psychiatrist in New Haven. Dieffy was a big Saint Bernard of a fellow, good-natured and sincere. He was as indignant as Bishop and told me that the class had held a rump meeting to discuss the matter. It had been decided to circulate a petition in favor of retaining the dismissed professor.

Nothing like this was going on in any of my classes, and I found myself very much interested. When the young biologists had had their petition rudely rejected, I found myself feeling as affronted as Bishop and Diefendorf. They had at least expected an audience with President Arthur Twining Hadley and a chance to present their case personally.

"Nothing to do now," muttered Dieffy, "but to write a letter to the *News*."

Impulsively, I took him up on his idea. "Let me write it for you," I told him.

When I got through with that letter, it was a masterpiece of venom and did everything but accuse the Biology Department of being German spies who had fired the innocent young instructor because he was about to expose them. I had, of course, no facts except those given me by Bishop and Diefendorf. But off we sent the letter.

And it was Henry Robinson Luce and the board of the *Yale Daily News* who decided to publish it—in full and prominently—with a pious editorial denouncing Bishop, Diefendorf, and Ingersoll as intemperates. Some enterprising heeler turned this inflammatory material in to a wire service, and it is a question whether the University or Bishop, Diefendorf, and Ingersoll were the more shocked and surprised the next day when the whole business turned up in the New York papers under a headline reading, STUDENTS ACCUSE YALE FACULTY OF PRO GERMAN LEANING.

The equivalent to the shock effect of this today would be for the *Harvard Crimson* to print a piece exposing President Pusey's membership in a Communist cell.

I never did meet Henry Robinson Luce in connection with this business—nor any other while I was in New Haven. He was not only an Academic student and a class ahead of me, but he was also a Big Man. As such—since he was not a gambling fellow—there was no reason for our paths ever to cross.

The end of the Biology Affair was unsatisfying for the assistant professor. We got him a temporary stay of execution, but they fired him in the end. It did wonderful things for me, however. When President Hadley, who stuttered, summoned the three of us to his sanctum, I was ready for him. I had never met Hadley before, but, because he was an old friend of my family, he singled me out for his attack.

"Ingersoll," he said, "I would like you to give me one single r-r-r-reason why I should not expel you, h-h-h-here and now!"

My appalling answer, given instantly and without hesitation, was, "Because you don't dare."

And he didn't, for he knew just as well as I that he would only be pouring kerosene on the fire I had started.

The technical device that the faculty employed to defeat their insurgent students was to order a formal investigation of the charges we had brought—and then to drag the hearings out until the academic year was over. As soon as we were gone our several ways for the summer, they let the poor professor go.

When I got back to New Haven the following fall, I was a full-fledged senior. Mercifully, however, I was saved from further adventures as an undergraduate by falling in love, this time for real. And by the same act, my career as an honor student was also upended. Just to show you what appalling things love can accomplish, let me tell the story.

In the fall term of my senior year I was one of a dozen students selected for a special class in Advanced Calculus. If I was not quite one of the mathematical geniuses, I could at least play in the same park with them. But within three months of my falling in love—it happened at about five minutes before eight in the doorway to an apartment in the East Sixties in New York—I had not merely succeeded in being dropped out of this class; I had fallen all the way to the bottom fringe of the moron classification—another specially selected class, conducted for the dullest-witted students in the whole university.

I did not make this descent intentionally. By this time I very definitely wanted to graduate, even with honors, so I worked conscientiously and hard. But I had just plain lost every vestige of the easy understanding I had once had. I now just plain knew that I could not understand things today that I knew I had understood yesterday. It was very, very disconcerting, and I thought seriously that I might be losing my mind.

Not that I really cared; all I wanted now was the girl who had opened the door to the apartment on Sixtieth Street.

IX · Sophistication Abroad

I courted Constance Clarke for not quite a year, during which period I graduated from college. In the emotional condition I was in, my graduation at all was miraculous; but to me it was inconsequential.

During the first six months, my courtship was uninterrupted, but after my commencement I got a few fortnights off, on parole for good behavior, so to speak. These weeks I spent grudgingly in Europe, as a kind of bodyguard and companion to Roland Mather Hooker.

The idea that I should make the Grand Tour with him after our graduation was his mother's, because I was somewhat unfairly considered a good influence on Poly. I had the same kind of reputation with Mrs. Hooker that I had had with the Emmets. I was the kind of boy who would see to it that Hooker wouldn't lose his tickets.

It was very painful for me to leave Constance, but I finally had her promise that she would marry me in the fall—as soon as I could support her. And she was emphatic that a summer in Europe, all expenses paid, was too important to pass up.

I would have passed it up in a minute. It was the sheerest physical and mental anguish to be separated from her. But Constance was the kind of a girl who made decisions for you, and you were stuck with them. So I consoled myself with thoughts of her constancy, and her unselfishness in sacrificing herself to the broadening of my education, and took ship with Hooker on a tiny French liner, the S. S. *Lorraine.*

Principally, these months were concerned with Hooker's own romance, of which I was to find myself General Manager. It began on the gangplank. Hooker, whom I regarded with great affection as being without a serious bone in his make-up—and who had always been pointedly uninterested in "nice" girls— announced suddenly, half way up this gangplank, that he had just decided to get married: to the girl in the big straw hat who was hanging over the railing just above us.

Neither of us had ever seen her before Hooker had looked up and caught her eye, or vice versa. Yet five weeks later I was to sail for home to plead his cause in this marriage, which was eventually to take place—though not before a succession of obstacles, each seeming at the time unsurmountable, was overcome.

But the first thing I had to do was to pick up an acquaintance with the girl herself, in order that I could present Hooker to her. He wanted it this way so that I could build him up before the introduction.

The girl turned out to be a young lady named Betty, traveling to Rome with her mother. They were to visit a relative there who had something to do with an American film company making a picture on location. Since Betty was a good-looking girl—slim and very blond—I smelled promotion and suspected her mother of having planned the trip to get Betty in pictures.

As for Betty and her mother, they took one look at Hooker and made no secret of *their* being unimpressed. Poly was hardly a young girl's notion of what Young Lochinvar should look like.

So, in my infinite sophistication, I decided that the only thing to do was to get this nonsense out of Hooker's head. Betty had no competition aboard the *Lorraine,* but when I got my friend to Paris . . .

The only immediate trouble was that now Hooker had in mind not going to Paris at all; he wanted me to radio for space on the same train that was taking Betty to Rome. So the best I could make was a deal that if Hooker would spend one week with me in Paris, at the end of that week I would go with him—if he still wanted to pursue the elusive Betty. With this I dismissed the subject, and went looking for my own trouble. I was confident that between Paris and Betty herself, we would cure him, for Betty had now taken to hiding in her cabin to avoid both of us.

The first place I looked for trouble was, of course, in the bar. Up until then, my bar life had been limited, and I was fascinated with the place. All the ship's most interesting characters were there, my favorite being a real cowboy with genuine bowlegs, who was returning to France with his war bride, to show Grandmamma their two-year-old child. Since the war bride preferred her cabin to the deck, the cowboy had custody of the child; and since the cowboy preferred the company of the bar to either, the child got to be well known there. To protect it from the hazards of the sea, the cowboy produced a lasso, with which he roped the child and tied it to the bar rail, where it greatly enjoyed life among the spittoons.

I myself was such a consistent patron that I soon became almost one of the ship's staff; and the bartender steward, having initiated me into what was then considered a dry Martini (one third was a mixture of French and Italian vermouth), often let me take over for him while he disappeared for relaxation of his own. It was great fun and the best way I'd found to keep my mind off Constance; but it was eventually to prove almost my undoing.

By the time we were within a few days of France, I had become so proprietary about the *Lorraine*'s tiny bar that I began to consider I had the right to choose its patrons. For instance, when the cowboy got *too* drunk, I would refuse to serve him; and I began to criticize the manners of other guests. Finally, one evening after dinner, when a too-handsome young man of about my own age said something to his girl that I didn't like, I suggested that *he* take *his* business elsewhere. When his not unreasonable reply was, "Where else is there to take it?" I found that this served only to increase my irritation.

Well, one remark like that led to another and the next thing you knew we were having a whale of a good fight out on deck, and drawing a pretty good crowd. And when the deck steward broke *that* one up, we repaired to the main salon on "A" deck and went at it again.

This latter site was poorly chosen. Presently we found ourselves desperately entwined, rolling down the full length of the grand staircase from "A" deck to "B." At this point we were met by no less than the Captain of the *Lorraine* himself. He had been sent for by the deck steward.

With the aid of a few of the Captain's sailors, we were disentangled. Our fellow passengers had been much too impressed by the show to care to interfere.

Hooker had arrived about the time of the Captain's appearance, and with his aid I retired to our cabin—to rest and refit, as the British military would put it. No really serious damage had been done, so as soon as my nose had stopped bleeding I put on some clean clothes and we returned to the grand salon—only to be met there by my late opponent. We might then have had another happy round of fisticuffs had it not been for the fact that my friend had chosen to return armed with a pistol. This time, even heretofore-neutral observers felt they should *do* something. They disarmed the poor fellow and returned him to his cabin.

For poor Poly this affair was the last straw. Publicly identified with such a ruffian as I, his reputation with Betty was now ruined beyond repair—and there was barely a nod in his direction when I led him meekly off the boat at Le Havre, Paris-bound.

Put to service as a distraction for my lovelorn friend, Paris couldn't have been more co-operative. It was the summer of 1921, and every boat train disgorged another load of merry-makers. A dollar would buy sixteen francs, which had only yesterday been worth twenty cents apiece and which still had nearly the same purchasing power. At ten francs a bottle, the most limited budget could buy champagne—and did.

For the American college boy on a spree, the day began at 5:00 P.M. at Harry's Bar and proceeded with an uninterrupted series of reunions in one bar, restaurant, or night club after another till six or seven in the morning. Then, of course, came the biggest reunion of all, when everyone showed up at Les Halles for a breakfast of coffee and brandy. These reunions might be with old friends—or even relatives, for *everyone* was in Paris that summer—but anyone whose face you'd ever seen before in America, or on the boat coming over, or even yesterday, was excuse enough for a happy celebration.

It was fortunate that I had a good constitution, because, in addition to such nights, I put in whole days tramping through museums. I wasn't going to miss *anything*. I did, however, get an hour or two of sleep each day between seven and nine in the morning—and might even have gotten in a nap in the late afternoon if this time had not been reserved for my daily letter to Constance.

At this period I thought of myself as suffering dreadfully from enforced separation. Actually, I am quite sure I was having a splendid time. Since Hooker seemed content to follow me any-

where I wished, except to a museum, it never occurred to me
that I was not through with his problem—until exactly midnight
of the seventh day he had promised to spend with me in Paris!

I can't remember how we happened to be there, but where
we were was on a park bench in the garden of the Tuileries. I
think we'd just left a house of ill fame. Everyone had to visit
such a place in Paris that summer; it was just something that
was *done*—if only as a voyeur. This of course was Poly's and
my own role; we would have felt unfaithful to our loves in any
other. As it was, it was bad enough, and we were as profoundly
shocked as we had expected to be. I think we walked down
from Montmartre to the rue de Rivoli and went into the park
to let some fresh air in on the experience.

Then suddenly Hooker was lighting a match to look at his
watch and rumbling, "Well, the time is up. You said you'd get
me to Rome. Now get me there."

My relationship with Hooker was like that. He was very real-
istic about his own inability to get anything he wanted done for
himself, and he had a childlike confidence that he had only to
ask me and I'd get it done for him. I had to explain to him that
it was still midnight and we would have to wait till the travel
agencies opened later in the morning.

"It's all right," said Hooker, "if you say so—but let's go sit on
its doorstep and wait for it to open."

That's the way Hooker was, too; so that's what we did. *The*
place was Cook's Wagon-Lit Bureau, which was on the Place
de la Madeleine. By the time we got there, the café across the
street was closed for the night, so we simply sat down on the
sidewalk to wait for *it* to open. Since we were clearly American,
passing gendarmes saw nothing odd in this, and neither did the
waiters who came around six to set out the sidewalk tables. They
volunteered that Cook's might open by nine. We had three hours
more to kill.

Throughout our vigil, Hooker was not only quiet, but calm.
It was only that his faith in me was so complete that I began

to feel some special effort on my part was indicated. Clearly I must contrive a gesture of some size to be worthy of him.

As is the custom, the waiters of the café stacked the saucers from each drink we ordered one upon the other, to keep the count for our bills. By nine o'clock, both piles were beginning to look like miniature towers of Pisa. But we were still able to see when Cook's doors at last swung open.

I've always enjoyed recalling our dignified entry and application to an immaculate British clerk in a morning coat.

"We would like," I said carefully, "transportation to Rome."

"Certainly," said the clerk. "The *good* night train leaves at eight—of course you *could* take an express around noon."

"Much too slow. Won't do at all," I informed him. And then came my inspiration. "By aeroplane," I added, "by *private* aeroplane, of course."

At that time, the only commercial travel by air was a hazardous transchannel trip which few dared to try. My hat is still off to the *sang-froid* with which Cook's representative handled my request.

"Certainly, sir," he answered, without batting an eyelash. "If you will excuse me a minute, I shall give you a quotation."

And that is all he took to come back with the figure of fifteen hundred dollars. Fifteen hundred dollars, then, might be five thousand now; even by de luxe *wagon-lit,* I expect we could have made the trip for a hundred dollars.

Soon after the first test pilot makes it from one continent to another by rocket, I look forward to putting it up to Cook's to charter me one for a junket to Timbuktu. The 1921 undertaking for which Cook's so casually assumed responsibility involved their setting up a relay of former military planes, to be flown by a succession of former combat pilots. These had to be recruited for the purpose. In the meantime they had to work out a route which led by successive hops from Paris to Dijon to Lyons, thence over the mountains to Nice and down the Mediterranean coast to Pisa, from which, it was hoped, Rome could be made in a single nonstop flight. The aircraft that were patched together for our use were baling-wire biplanes; they had open cockpits seating three in tandem.

All this, in Hooker's name, for the love of a young lady who wouldn't give him the time of day! But just wait until we swooped down on her in our aeroplane to the applause of a gathered multitude! It didn't bother us in the least that, airborne on 1921 wings, we would take three days to complete a journey we could have made by train in one.

I have an extensive photographic record of this trip, made with a three-A Kodak lent by my family for cultural purposes. The flight was now such a big thing that it almost made me forget Constance.

We took off from Le Bourget—the field Lindbergh was to land on six years later—and the first plane got us as far as Dijon, where we landed in a vacant lot. Another plane was waiting there. In this we made Lyons by nightfall.

Since at Lyons we were well on our way—we had covered a whole two hundred and ninety miles—we were enormously exhilarated. We drove to town in style and retired to what we were told was Lyons' best hotel, to rest for the morrow. A special plane was being flown in for this leg of the flight, on which we had to climb to a very great altitude to surmount the Alps. But even before that, we had to surmount the obstacle that Lyons itself was to become.

At "the best hotel" in Lyons, I engaged the only accommodation that seemed appropriate for Hooker: the bridal suite. This was an enormous affair of crystal and lace with huge French doors opening onto a court. These doors we flung wide, and retired in haste, since it had now been something like thirty-six hours since we had had even a cat nap. Moreover, we were a little short of sleeping equipment because our luggage had been forwarded by express. You couldn't expect a plane to carry three people *and* luggage. But it was a hot July night, and so neither of us minded sleeping in the nude.

It must have been around two or three in the morning before I found out what was wrong with this arrangement. I was still three-quarters unconscious, but I knew what was biting me: mosquitoes, millions of mosquitoes. They were pouring into the bridal suite through the open French doors.

I got a bed lamp turned on to look for cover, and the sight it illumined horrified me wide awake. Mosquitoes I do not like; happily they are not very fond of me either. But clearly they adored Hooker. And, as clearly, he was allergic to them. In the bed next to me where he lay naked, Hooker had swollen, from head to foot, to almost twice his natural size. His face bore no resemblance to anything human. It was a ball of purple dough with both eyes welded tight shut. His lips and throat were so swollen that I could barely hear the sounds he must have been trying to make in a pathetic plea for help; his bloated arms were threshing about as if trying to beckon.

There was no time to stop to reason. This was serious business. I ran out into the hall and began shouting at the top of my lungs. I have a confused memory of managers and managers' wives appearing in night clothes, and of bellboys arriving, still pulling on pants. Even the pilot turned up, and there was an enormous conference, the gist of which was denied me by my ignorance of French. I simply kept shouting for a doctor, any kind of a doctor.

The conference was soon broken up by a stream of orders emerging from the manager of the hotel. It is possible that he had had a similar experience with other guests, for he seemed to know exactly what to do. The iceboxes of the hotel were rifled for their full supply of blocks of ice, which were hastily chipped and shredded until a whole bathtub full of cracked ice was at hand. A dozen willing hands lifted the naked Hooker from his bed of pain, carried him to the tub, and packed him in the ice—head, hands, feet, and all.

And then we prayed. And, by golly, it worked! With the dawn light, Hooker (mercifully still alive) was seen to have shrunk back to something roughly resembling his original size. Of course, the shrinkage was not entirely even and it left him a most peculiar splotch-work of purple and white; but he now mumbled words that were almost intelligible and his eyes were open a full eighth of an inch.

We carried him back to bed and thawed him out with hot-water bottles. By 8:00 A.M. Hooker could even stand up, and by nine we completed his revival with a pint of brandy. He now made motions indicating his anxiety to continue the flight.

The flight? The flight to his loved one's side! But, my God, what a terrible-looking lover I now had on my hands! The shoemaker's stepdaughter wouldn't have taken him with a dowry of a million dollars. But he would have it no other way than that we continue.

We got over the mountains all right. The altitude must have had a good effect on Hooker, for he slept soundly the whole way, wedged and strapped into the cockpit in front of us. This was the thing our new pilot found hardest to understand.

"*Mon Dieu,*" he kept repeating, "you tell me he is paying for this trip. How can he be paying and not stay awake to enjoy it?"

The pilot concerned—the last of our relay team—was a genuine war hero and the survivor of a hundred successful encounters with the Boche. He had not, however, come through quite unscathed. He told me that the vibrations of a plane still opened up old wounds and knotted the muscles of his neck so badly that he had to telegraph ahead, on each leg of the journey, to have a masseur standing by to unknot him when he descended.

Greatly as I admired his courage in continuing to fly, I admit to wondering what would happen to us if we were delayed an extra hour or two in the air. I asked him once, and he said that it was not for me to worry because none of the planes we flew in carried gasoline enough for us to stay in the air an extra hour. Fifteen or twenty minutes, that was always possible. . . .

At Nice, we spent an afternoon and a night completing Poly Hooker's recovery—the recovery of his more important working

parts, that is; it was literally weeks before his features were
wholly returned to him.

Our only other real adventure on that trip was a much happier
one. Toward noon of the third day, we dropped out of a cloudless
sky onto the military airport at Pisa. It was, after all, the only
airport available. Here, and here alone, had Cook's arrangements
gone astray. Since we had no clearance there, nor any papers
permitting us entry into this foreign land, all three of us were
in the process of being marched off to the hoosegow when our
famous pilot somehow made himself understood. In World War
I, Italy was our faithful ally, and our pilot's reputation was so
famous that even the Italian officers recognized his name. So
instead of being herded into the calaboose, we were asked to
lunch—and what a lunch it turned out to be!

The entire garrison of Italian officers was rounded up—there
were fifty or sixty of them—mess tables were covered with shining
linen, and champagne was sent for from town. The Italian Air
Force knew well how to rise to an occasion.

Before they had done with us, even Hooker and I were in the
act. Information had reached Pisa that the latest American dance
step was known as "Le Shimmy," and that no one could think
of himself as a man of the world until he had mastered it. "Ah,
but you are Americans and you will know!" After the second
bottle of champagne, I found that I did—and it was a great pleasure for me to instruct our allies. Standing on a speaker's dais,
I directed the shoulder movements of several score of nattily
uniformed Italian aviators, to the accompaniment of a piano
and an accordion.

It was not at Pisa that our pilot needed the ministrations of
a masseur; after three bottles of champagne he demonstrated his
mastery over the laws of gravity all the way from Pisa to Rome.
Since the maneuvers he chose to demonstrate it included a chandelle, several slow rolls between the spires of a cathedral, and
much buzzing of beaches to admire the young ladies, it was quite
a ride. The chandelle is a take-off stunt in which the pilot ex-

ecutes a backward loop as soon as he has gained flying speed; he comes back over the field hanging from his safety belt and then flips the plane right side up in front of the grandstand. It used to be a saying in World War I circles that the chandelle may be a beautiful thing to watch but unfortunately all the *good* chandelle pilots are dead.

We were, then, in very fine form for our triumphant arrival in Rome. There, at least, we were sure that Cook's had told them we were coming. But Rome is more sophisticated than Pisa, and our only reception committee consisted of two mechanics who'd been waiting grumpily for us to get in. Nor had even a car been provided for our entry into the imperial city itself. So the end of the long, long trail from the Place de la Madeleine to Rome was hanging for our lives to the sides of the only transportation available, an overcrowded open streetcar.

A very ignominious business, that! But I could still count several thousand dollars of Hooker's money in my pocket. With these I could set up such a shop in Rome as would *really* dazzle the lady in the straw hat. And Hooker still had confidence that I was the boy who could do it for him.

There were several reasons why it seemed important that I should count Hooker's money. The first was Hooker's *idée fixe* that he had only his money to recommend him to Betty. His own opinion of himself had never been very high.

The second reason was that once our traveling funds had been spent, he would be at the mercy of his mother—and Mother's good opinion of Poly's decision to marry was anything but in the bag. He had not had time to hear from her, but he had no confidence in what she would say when he did. She had never trusted Hooker's judgment in anything, and besides, he would have to write her that Betty's family were devout Roman Catholics. He had a vague idea that his Episcopal parents would not approve of that.

We were hardly settled in the biggest suite that the Hotel

Excelsior had for rent before Hooker's worst fears were confirmed—by a blunt cable from Hartford. In view of the nature
of Hooker's proposed alliance, it read, no more funds would be
forthcoming. And Betty was as adamant as ever that she had
no intention of marrying Hooker anyway. It was going to be a
long siege. So we began our debate as to what to do next.

I had come a long way around since writing off Hooker's
attachment as an infatuation. I was all for him now and, being
in love myself, could imagine no more horrible fate than his. I
was angry with Betty for rejecting my friend and angrier still
with his mother for being so shortsighted about her son's welfare.
Good lord, Poly had even gone on the wagon since arriving in
Rome!

Meanwhile, this whole steeped-in-love atmosphere was making
my own loneliness for Constance unbearable. Rome was almost
as gay as Paris, and the days were endlessly long and sunny;
they made a mockery of Constance's not being with me. So I
ended the debate and my own agony by deciding to take the
next ship home, to tackle Mrs. Hooker personally. Hooker was
to be left in the siege lines, with instructions to conserve his
ammunition until I could arange resupply.

Sped home on the wings of my own love, it was the work of
but a single hour's passionate exposition to bring poor Mrs.
Hooker around to her son's side. I ran her down in her own drawing room in Hartford, there to make my first and most effective
plea for religious tolerance. The Hookers, like many a New England family, were traditionally antipapist; but a refunding cable
was on its way to Hooker before I left.

The end of Hooker's love story was that, after sweating out
the rest of the summer in Rome, he still had to follow Betty and
her mother back to America before she broke down. But she
finally did.

This was long after I had gone west to the mines, so I wasn't
even at the wedding. I think I was named godfather to their first
son, who looks remarkably like his father now and was a naval

aviator of some distinction in World War II. So, some good came of it all.

As for me, after Mrs. Hooker had sent her cable, I was on the first combination of trains that would take me from Hartford to Quebec.

I was off to Quebec because Constance had been spending the summer there—with *her* mother, at a place called Murray Bay, which is on the St. Lawrence, out toward its mouth. Ahead of me, of course, had gone cables to announce my impending arrival. It was still August, and we would have a month together before I was due to report to the North Star Mining and Development Company's local office in Grass Valley, which is in Nevada County, California. There, I had been assured before my graduation from Yale, I had a job of some kind waiting for me.

It was a lucky break, lining up any kind of a job in the mining profession that year, because half the mines in the country were shut down. In 1921, there was a walloping little economic depression on. Most people have forgotten what happened three years after the end of World War I. The market for copper and lead and zinc had gone to blazes, but that only made gold the more valuable, and gold was what they mined in Grass Valley.

So, I was off to the happy ending of my own love story: to my impatiently waiting fiancée and a happy month together making plans for a wedding.

I should have valued that train ride more, because on it I was to pass the last happy hours of my relationship with Constance Clarke. I got the bad news officially after dinner the first night. Constance had "had time to think it over" while I'd been abroad. If I had to know—and she hated horribly to tell me— she had in the meantime become engaged to marry someone else.

There was one really nice thing about Constance: when she told you that her mind was made up, you knew darned well it was.

As I remember, the night train back left around eight. I was on it.

x · Ah, Love!

For many years the thing that interested me about my having been so in love with Constance Clarke was that I never liked her. When she was most obviously in love with me, and most gracious and almost, though never quite, dependent on me for her own happiness, I *still* didn't like her. She had a hard, brash quality. There was a kind of bossiness about her which reminded me of everything I had found unattractive in my sisters.

She had also a sudden explosive unmusical laugh, which was

her reaction to anything in the least unusual or out of the ordinary. What displeased her, she would dismiss with an imperious *pshaw;* and she had a temper when she was crossed. Also, she was a social snob of the first order.

Of all these characteristics, I was entirely aware—literally within a few hours after we had met. Even so, my knowledge of them came too late. I had fallen wholly and completely in love with Constance the second I laid eyes on her. She had answered the door herself, on my arrival for a dinner she was giving. I didn't know her and had never heard of her, for she'd only just moved from Baltimore to New York. A girl I did know had been invited to her dinner, and had brought me.

I can see Constance now, standing there smiling, telling us to come in. She was very beautiful, with swept-back blond hair, so light in color that it was almost platinum. Her severely classical features were set in an attractively broad face. Her eyes were the color of ice reflecting a very blue sky on a sunny day; and her skin and her coloring were so good that even at the height of her career as a Beauty she used no make-up.

Love's tendency to blindness is supposed to be most marked in the very young, but I can't ever remember being more alert and wide awake than I was when I was falling in love with Constance. I knew, by the time I'd come in and taken off my overcoat, that she was my whole life and that whatever she turned out to be I was stuck with. And by the end of the evening I knew that what I was stuck with was a female whom I just plain didn't like.

There really isn't much to the story from here on. We had met during a Thanksgiving holiday. After that I was with her every weekend in New York. As soon as I had a good solid two weeks at Christmas to work with, I got her to agree to marry me.

There was never any talk about running away to get married, or of getting married secretly right then and there. It was my stubborn belief that a man should not take a wife until he could support her. I guess Father had sneaked that idea into my head.

So, I simply gave her a gold ring with a tiny diamond in it—one that I'd inherited from some relative or other—and we considered ourselves committed.

There is a peculiar pattern in my life. Catastrophe has invariably been followed—and quite promptly—by something wholly unforeseen but very good happening to me. And so it was almost immediately after Constance's rejection, which I most seriously considered as the end of any kind of life worth living.

It took me a round five years to get over Constance. As late as four and a half years after Murray Bay, I saw her walking on Madison Avenue, a block and a half away from me, and was so overcome by emotion at the distant sight of her that I had to turn and hurry away. Yet during those five years I had been extremely active.

At the end of five years, all these emotions—and the assumptions based on them—simply evaporated. They dissolved like a heavy fog in the warmth of the sun. It was just that one day something reminded me of her and I was startled by the realization that I had not thought of her for months. So, just because I was curious, I sought her out; she was never hard to find. And what I suspected was true; my soul was my own again.

But during those five years I never ceased to be vulnerable, knowing always that she had only to walk into my life again to make everything else in it seem unimportant—and me miserable.

How much worse it might have been but for the good thing that happened to me, I will never know. I *have* been so depressed, in my lifetime, that I have lain all night clenching bedposts with white knuckles, for fear I would still do what I thought I wanted to, which was to jump out a window—a window a dozen stories too high for a casual gesture. But the shock of losing Constance never cost me a night like that, I have always thought, because an extremely nice girl saw to it that it couldn't.

Her name was Jeannine, and she was my first adventure in having someone fall in love with me before I fell in love with her. When Jeannine fell in love with me, all I felt was gratitude—and pity.

That in itself was to have its effect on me. It got me all mixed up on the subject of love in general. Here were Constance and I: the more deeply I felt toward her, the less impression I had seemed to make—until I had become intolerable to her. The same thing, with the sexes reversed, happened to Jeannine and me. Was I to conclude that that was the rule? That to be loved, one must withhold love? And, conversely, that to love intensely, without reservation of any kind, was to make oneself undesirable? Was love, then, generated only by the challenge of disinterest?

At twenty years of age, I did indeed so conclude; and since to be loved when one felt no response was its own form of torture, I wrote the whole equation off as insoluble and saw no future in it.

The psychiatrist will recognize the pattern easily enough. I was arranging my life to protect myself from the one relationship I could not bear to face: fulfilled love. Fulfilled love could remind me only of what I had so desperately wanted as a child and yet known was forbidden: fulfillment of my love for my mother.

So I first arranged to love only someone who could not return my love, and then got someone to love me at a time when I could feel no deep response. Then I concluded—on the incontrovertible evidence that I had manufactured myself—that the whole experience was inherently unsatisfactory. Anyone with sense would avoid it like a plague. My psychological self-castration was now complete.

And that is the way it happened, I believe, because after Jeannine there was no sex at all in my life—no sex with love—for, oh, one, two, three, maybe four years. This could have cost me my confidence in myself—as a man who could be loved—but for the memory of the single night that was Jeannine's.

This is the story of it.

I had just come home from Murray Bay to Father's and Tante's farm in Salisbury, too savagely silent for my family to dare invade the privacy of my grief. I mowed the lawn for them, and chopped wood for their fireplaces, in tight-lipped obedience to their slightest request. To my father, I was still the small boy—six feet three inches tall—whose character would benefit from chores assigned and well done. But within the fortnight I would be going away for good and all, to earn my own living. Therefore, Father would make a concession to the occasion. "The boy"—I was so referred to until the day he died, when I was almost fifty—"the boy" could take "the car" whenever he wished, every night if it pleased him. It was "the car"—a shiny new touring job with a canvas top, a 1920 Dodge, I think—that brought Jeannine and me together.

The Dodge took me, when the still and starry nights became intolerable at the farm, for lonely drives afield. Out on the graveled back roads which I knew so well, I could draw up into the shadows of tall hemlocks and let my mind go blank, giving my body to the waves of pain that welled up in me, beyond my control, beyond my comprehension. And after it was over, and the nausea was gone, I could start up again—because what else was there that I *could* do—and drive on, the cool night air comforting me.

On one such drive, after a spell that I thought would never end, I became frightened of being alone and I drove into the village. There was a country dance in progress there, in an empty schoolhouse. I went in. The light and the warmth felt good, and I sat down on a bench by the wall to listen to the music.

I knew almost everyone there. They were the boys and girls I had grown up with, more or less, ever since my father had married Tante when I was fifteen and had come to live in Salisbury. Only I had never been around them for long—just enough to know who was who, and for them to know who I was. A few of the girls I had kissed a few times and thought I had been very daring.

Now none of them seemed even grown; they danced awkwardly, in starched party dresses, and looked curiously at me as they passed. I was already kind of a character to the Salisbury people. I was one of them because my stepmother had local roots, yet a stranger because I had not really grown up there, and I'd been away so much, at college and even abroad. They were casting me in a romantic role, I thought wryly, and it made me uncomfortable. So I was about to go away again when Jeannine spoke to me.

I hadn't noticed her when I had come in; I had sat down next to her simply because there was space there on the bench. She asked me who I was, and I told her, noticing that she wasn't one of the village group. I had never seen her before. She was in her twenties, to the others' teens, a woman, rather than a girl, with dark hair and very large brown eyes and a very full sensuous mouth.

"This is pretty bad," she said to me, suddenly. "You have a car, haven't you?"

I said that I had, and we went for the drive she asked of me. It didn't matter much.

After a while, when I had no conversation whatever to contribute, Jeannine had me drive her up a lonely bypass which led to a deserted race track. It was on a hill overlooking the town. We stopped there.

After we stopped, Jeannine said speculatively, "You're carrying a torch, aren't you? Tell me about it."

I couldn't see any reason why not. It would be interesting to see whether I *could* tell it now, to a stranger. I wondered if it would make any sense to her.

So that's how it began—and it went on like that, with me talking about myself, and Jeannine listening, for six nights. Each evening I would pick her up at her house after supper and each night I would bring her back at three or four—once even at five—in the morning. It didn't matter.

Jeannine asked, and I offered, nothing but my conversation; but by the time we were done, the sting was out of my hurt and I knew I was beginning to get well again.

What a very, very patient girl she was! Dear God, think of having to listen, all those hours, to a lovesick young man talking about himself! I was grateful to her and, as I came to my senses, apologetic. So the last few nights I was almost gay, trying to make it up to her for having suffered with me. I began telling her stories that I thought would amuse her, about Hooker in Europe and the 360 Club and such trivia.

I remember being conscious for the first time that she was a very attractive woman, and admiring her dark coloring. "You would look well in a very strong red," I told her once, thinking of the pastel shades the very blonde Constance so often wore. Everything about Jeannine seemed Constance's opposite.

After Jeannine and I found that we could laugh as well as cry together, it could have gone on for sixty nights as easily as six. But there was always that deadline by which I had to leave for California; there was no changing that.

Jeannine didn't talk about herself, and I could have been no more than polite if she had. My sorrow made me arrogant, and I had no interest in her except as an audience. She might have been in the back seat instead of beside me; once started, I would have gone right on talking, as if to an unseen analyst.

So when the week was over, it was as if I had had no personal conversation at all with Jeannine; but I felt very close to her and knew that she felt close to me. I was surprised to recognize that I would be really sorry to leave her. A week before, all I could think of was getting away as fast as I could—as far away as I could from anything that I had ever known before.

I was to start my journey west on a train for Chicago that left Grand Central Station around eleven in the morning. I would have to say good-by to Jeannine *two* nights before, because to make the connection meant leaving Lakeville in the afternoon and spending the night in New York.

It was that last night in Salisbury that we sat up so very, very late, and Jeannine asked if my family were going to New York to see me off.

I said, "Good lord, no! They will drive me as far as the station in Millerton, and be so embarrassed about saying good-by that they won't even wait for the train to come in. You're New England enough yourself to know that."

"You'll be leaving for the down train a little before three, won't you?"

"Let's see," I said, "the train leaves at 3:20 and the station is a good seven miles from the farm. My father will want the baggage in the car by 2:30; and the oil and gas checked—and his formal farewell speech finished—by 2:45. So we will start for the station at exactly 2:50. I can see that you haven't been around my family much," I added. "We run automobiles like railways where I come from."

In point of fact, my father's speech was over at 2:44. It had been brief and to the point: "You are going out to California to start your career at the bottom of the ladder, boy. I envy you. Remember as you climb, boy, that there is always room at the top"—which I thought singularly appropriate words to a young man about to disappear into a mine.

It was not until 2:46 that the party-line phone rang our number and the operator asked for me by name, for a call from New York. It was Jeannine. I was startled to realize that she must have gone down on the morning train.

She spoke rapidly and to the point. "I don't want to talk on the telephone. When you get to New York, walk right on through the station and go into the Commodore Hotel. Just ask the man at the desk there for the key to Mrs. Rogers' suite. Not Mrs. Martin's, Mrs. Rogers'! That's all you have to do. Can you remember?"

I thought, irritably, "Jeannine, too, thinks of me as a child—giving me directions how to get across Grand Central Station! What does she think I am?"

But she had hung up before I could remonstrate—or ask her about this Mrs. Rogers with whom she was staying. Jeannine had said nothing about her visiting in New York when we'd said good-by.

I really was that innocent.

Next day, I caught the train west by seconds.

XI · In and Under California

The town of Grass Valley is in California's Nevada County—the one that sticks into the State of Nevada, opposite Reno. It is way, way up in the tall-tree-covered mountains, only a county or two away from the one in which they first found gold in 1849.

Gold in that county came from a formation called the Mother Lode. There are the same kind of formations underground around Grass Valley—deeply imbedded veins of quartz intruded into solid granite.

A vein, geologically speaking, is not at all the kind of thing you have in your arm and which bleeds when you cut it. It is more like the slice of meat in a sandwich—the meat being the gold-bearing quartz and the bread the granite. In Grass Valley the sandwich-meat-slices of quartz are not horizontal, but slant down into the bread loaf of granite at an angle of about forty-five degrees—mostly. They run down as far as you can follow them—seven or eight thousand feet—and they vary greatly in width, from a few inches to a score or more feet.

The gold in the quartz is usually in such minute particles that you cannot see it; but sometimes there are nuggets, from the size of a pinhead up to—well, I have never seen one as big as the end of my little finger. The gold the forty-niners first found was in flakes in the gravel bed of streams which had eroded the Mother Lode where its vein emerged on the surface. After this supply was exhausted, they had to begin digging out the veins themselves, each year going deeper.

By the time I got to Grass Valley, seventy-two years later, they were down in the veins there to the seven-thousand-foot level, which is down to where it is hotter than a man can work comfortably, because the temperature rises about one degree for every one hundred feet you dig down.

The way you get this kind of ore out of rock is to sink a vertical shaft until you intersect the vein—if you've got a smart geologist and you *do* intersect it, a mile down and out of sight. It *can* be missed altogether, for its slope and thickness are whimsical.

The last shaft they had sunk at Grass Valley before I got there had not only picked up the vein where it was supposed to, but had broken through into a pocket so rich in nuggets that the directors of the company themselves went down in buckets, with picks and shovels, to spend happy hours prying them loose. But after this pocket was exhausted, it was several years (and a couple of bond issues) later before they found any more. Gold mining is sometimes like that.

After you have found the vein, the next thing you do is called "blocking out the ore body." This entails burrowing out from either side of the shaft, and up and down, until you have blocked out as much of the meaty ore as you think you can digest, or have been able to find. The burrows will be a standard five feet wide and seven feet high, and when they run through ore, they are called "drifts," and through barren rock, "crosscuts." These drifts and crosscuts will go out at intervals up and down the shaft and, since engineers have nice orderly minds, these will always be one hundred feet apart and each will be known as a "level." So where you would speak of your office as being on the twelfth floor, a miner would refer to his working place as on, say, the forty-seven-hundred level, that is, forty-seven hundred feet below the surface. And the levels will be connected together by interior shafts called "raises." All this effort is just to get at the ore. The places where it is actually mined are called "stopes."

The process by which the solid rock is carved away under-ground—whether in shafts, drifts, raises, or stopes—is a very simple one. You drill little round holes in the face of the rock, fill the ends of them with dynamite, remove yourself from the vicinity, and set off one hole after another in succession. If you prescribe the right dosage, the dynamite not only breaks out the rock, but also breaks it up into small-enough pieces for you to shovel. Of course, every single shovelful has to be taken out of the mine it-self—thrown down chutes to be trammed to the shaft, and then hauled to the surface—every shovelful of rock whether there is gold in it or there isn't.

The little holes—two inches in diameter—which begin all this process, are chipped out with steel bits hammered in by com-pressed air drills which weigh one hundred and eighty pounds and strike four hundred blows to the minute. The man who runs one is called a "miner" and the man who shovels up the ore after he has broken it is described on the payroll as a "mucker."

At Grass Valley, a miner was what I yearned to be and a mucker was what I was for the first six months—at three dollars and seventy-five cents for every eight-hour day I was physically capable of putting in.

I write it that way because for the first few months I could rarely get more than three or four days in, in succession, before I would collapse with a combination of exhaustion and acute bronchitis, laryngitis, sinusitis, and the common cold. These were my reactions to working myself into a wringing perspiration and then cooling out in the fog of expanding compressed air that was the exhaust from the drill ahead of me.

The only thing I burned with those months—besides fever— was a passionate stubbornness about not quitting. On the mornings when I couldn't make it to the mine, I would rest a while and then make myself go for as long a walk as I could stand, through the lovely woods on the surface, to try at least to toughen my leg muscles, and to breathe the dry mountain air. Since the sun was almost always shining, on top, after a day or two I could usually manage another few shifts underground.

In this manner I gradually began to toughen up, until I could first hold my own and then begin savagely to compete with other muckers in other stopes for tonnage records. And then for the first time I began to look around me, and to enjoy myself immensely.

The memory that has haunted me most about life underground —at least in Grass Valley—is how beautiful the lights and shadows seemed to be. The light is from your own carbide lamp, and it is white and makes dramatic shadows that are never still. Often the newly broken quartz reflected the light and made its own patterns. The exhaust from the big drills, which I found so hard to breathe, condensed as it erupted and made weird fog effects.

And the miners working their drills I found beautiful, too, silhouetted against the rock. They were always in movement, for the great drills had to be wrestled with as they were wound into the holes they cut. They were fed water as well as air—to make sludge out of the quartz dust—so that a miner was characteristically drenched, with his shirt clinging to the great muscles of his shoulders, often so powerful that they seemed almost deformed. The man I worked with first *was* deformed, a huge hunchback of a German who could move his drill, mount and all, with either arm alone, the whole assembly weighing over two hundred and fifty pounds.

It is a shame that the hard-rock miner has never had a Bellows or a Marsh to immortalize him. He is a much more picturesque character than a prize fighter and just as rugged, and he lays not only his skill but his life on the line in violent action every day instead of once every few months, or years.

I am talking about the *hard-rock* miner, who considers himself a cut above the coal miner. The latter's opponent, in nature, is of softer substance—more treacherous, with its explosive gases, and possibly more dangerous—but not in itself the challenge to brute force that are the granites, quartzes, and hard porphyries in which the hard-rock miner works.

When he is coming off shift and in the change room, the hard-rock miner would be equally exciting to an artist. There he is stripped naked by the suspicion of the mine owner, and splashes in communal showers and happy horseplay. The young men are as beautifully proportioned as the sculpture of the ancient Greeks, and the bodies of the older men are like studies Michelangelo might have made.

The stripping process is, of course, unique with gold (and diamond) mines, and the routine is almost comic. The lockers where you hang your clothes are grappling hooks, to be hauled high up toward the rafters. After your work clothes are aloft, and you have scrubbed off the grime, you lower your street clothes down from their grappling hooks—all under watchful eyes.

If, despite these precautions, you have succeeded in smuggling some nuggets belonging to your employer, you are what is known as a "highgrader." If later you are caught, no jury in the country would consider it sporting to convict you. It would be hard to catch you anyway, because if you know what you're doing you have a little claim of your own up in the hills which you work yourself on Sundays—and simply turn in the stolen high-grade ore as coming from your own diggings. Among the Cornish miners in Grass Valley it was knowingly whispered that all the houses on one side of a certain street in London had been built with high-grade from the Valley.

I had fun underground, too, after I was acclimated and trained down to one hundred and seventy-five pounds of muscle and bone. Mostly I worked with these same Cornishmen, who loved a story so much that when someone told a good one every one of the group of listeners was supposed to retell it, competitively, each with his own variations. This would be in the half-hours off for lunch, when you would be heating coffee in the bottom of your dinner pail with the stub of a candle and the men would come down the ladders from stopes nearby and gather round to make themselves at ease on scraps of planks. This was when everyone felt good and the cousins began to concentrate on amusing each other.

The Cornishmen in California were always called "Cousin Jacks"—I know no reason why. Most of the miners in Grass Valley were Cousin Jacks because that's the way the town started —by the importation of a whole village of Cornish silver miners. In Cornwall they had been bred miners rather than trained. It almost seemed as if, after centuries of life underground, the process of natural selection had been at work. For their very bodies were functional—short, thickset, with heavy shoulders and practically no necks.

The art of the Cousin Jack as a miner had been passed down from father to son, I expect from before the Middle Ages. Transplanted six thousand miles, their custom was the same. When Johnny was fourteen or fifteen, his father asked permission of the superintendent to take Johnny down with him. Then Johnny went to work, not on the payroll, of course, but under his father's sternest discipline. His standards met, after months—or it could be years—Father simply waited on the foreman a second time, saying, "Jan's ready." And Johnny was.

It could be that all this is changed now, because terrible things had already begun to happen way back in 1921: every now and then an Americanized Johnny didn't choose to go down in the mine with Father, but simply took off instead, down the highway toward the coast. And then there would be a great shaking of heads underground, and a sadness that the old way was passing. But father training son was the order rather than the exception in my time.

I have spoken of mining being an art, but so is mucking, picking up broken rock with a long-handled shovel underground. Try to force your muckstick into a pile of broken quartz and then to lift it with your muscles alone; even if you're an athlete and in training, you will exhaust yourself within the hour. But when you have perfect balance and control, you can do it all day, although you will still have no time to daydream, for every thrust into broken rock must be analyzed lest you wedge yourself into something immovable—a sensation not unlike stubbing your toe at full gallop.

You can see from the above that I came to take my accomplishments as a mucker very seriously. I got an enormous satisfaction out of my first—and only—success as an athlete. Despite this, from my first month on, I never ceased to nag both the miner and the foreman who were my superiors for a chance at one of the big drills. I had no papa to instruct me, but now and then I'd get someone to let me put in a hole for him, in rock that didn't look too complicated.

These were prized concessions, grudgingly given, because I had but to get a six-foot drill half an inch out of line and the steel would be so wedged that it would take a master miner an hour to get it out—or he might have to abandon the hole, the drill stem stuck for good, and drill another next to it. Since every man on shift in a mine is racing against a deadline—the hour at which the blasting must be done—letting an eager amateur touch your machine is not a favor lightly given.

I went to work in September; it was well into spring, as I remember, before I made the grade and got a machine of my own —at four dollars and fifty cents a day, instead of three seventy-five.

I never did master a miner's trade. To be really good at it takes years of experience with an infinite variety of hardnesses and formations of rock. In my impatient ambition I had most definitely bought a pair of shoes too big for me. Hardly a shift went by that I did not have to impose on the patience of some professional in a neighboring stope to get me out of a jam I'd gotten myself into by my own ineptness, with wedged drills, tumbled setups, and lost holes. I expect—the way we used to look upon getting Pullian through the examinations in New Haven—it got to be a sporting matter on my shift to help me pass myself off as a journeyman miner. I can remember a hundred helpful things done for me without my asking, and without comment or reproach. And I never failed to have the word passed to me when the foreman was on his way in, so that I could tidy up and be ready for him.

After not too many weeks, all this undeserved attention began to prey on my mind, and I commenced to look around for some honorable way out. The way I found at last was to apply for a turn on something known as the reblast shift. This took a miner's knowledge of handling dynamite, but required no drilling. The loading and firing of holes had been the only part of the miner's job that I'd really mastered.

To understand the nuances of my application, you have a fact or two to master first. It takes two eight-hour shifts to drill the holes and to blast a round. The blasting is always the last thing done by the night shift, which loads and fires its holes and comes on top at midnight. After each miner has lit the fuses to his round—he may have loaded fifteen to twenty holes—he waits in the drift below his stope to hear them fire. He counts concussions carefully—the sound, through solid rock, like the taps of a hammer on the floor upstairs—and on his way out he reports to the shift boss how many of the holes actually went off. Sometimes they all went; sometimes one or more hung fire.

If there *is* a miss, the miner cannot go back to see what's the matter; the working stope is now filled with the dead gas of spent explosives. But somebody, sometime, *has* to go back, and go before the day shift comes back to work. The fellow who does is the reblast man.

The reblaster is the mine's demolition expert, the fellow who in World War II was sent for to take the fuses out of the bombs that didn't go off. His working equipment is a gunny sack of dynamite sticks over one shoulder and a pocket full of fulminate-of-mercury caps, and fuses in the other pocket; these things, and a six-foot steel rod with a spoonlike scraper on the end to fish the unexploded dynamite out of the unexploded holes, for each must be cleaned before being reloaded and reblasted.

It was not a job for which men were standing in line, even though, as I remember, it paid time and a half because of the graveyard hours—midnight to 8:00 A.M. So when I heard there was an opening and asked for it, it was most graciously given.

Theoretically, reblasting is the most dangerous of all underground activities, principally because holes sometimes go off after they've hung fire for hours. But no one ever got killed in this line of work while I was there; and it was my idea, at the time, that the job improved the odds on my survival. Most mine accidents seemed to me to come from someone else's carelessness, but on the reblast shift I worked alone, all alone, in a mine empty on the levels assigned to me.

It was often interesting work, reblasting, since it gave me a chance to study several dozen different working places instead of spending all my time in one stope. And it was a satisfyingly responsible job for a boy, because the lives of the shift that followed depended on the thoroughness of my work. If I missed a hole and the next day shift drilled into it, there was no question at all about what would happen to them.

Really the only trouble with the job was the almost unbearable headaches it gave you. The physical effects of handling nitroglycerine are highly dramatic. The chemical is absorbed through the pores of the skin and produces, almost immediately, the sensation that your skull is being severed just above the eyebrows, as by a wire being intolerably tightened.

Blasting dynamite is nitroglycerine in a gelatinous substance with the consistency of putty. Sticks of it are encased in waxed paper, but when you blast with it you slit this paper with a penknife. Then when you tamp half a dozen sticks into a hole, the stuff will ooze together into a single explosive amalgam. When you spend most of eight hours slitting sticks of dynamite and stuffing them in holes, you absorb a good deal of nitroglycerine; after the first hour, the resulting headache is almost as much as you can stand.

Aspirin is a specific for this kind of headache, but you grow to tolerate aspirin almost as fast as you increase the dosage, until you can take two hundred and fifty grains of it, by the handfuls of five-grain tablets, swallowed whole, without its having more than a slight dulling effect. Since nitroglycerine is a heart stimulant and aspirin a heart depressant, I suppose the two of them fight it out and leave you in the end where you began. But I recall the headaches as a major nuisance underground—and they went on for hours after I got on top, wearing off only slowly as I breathed pure air again.

I was a busy fellow, those days. The shifts I worked were eight hours long; add an hour to each end to walk the two miles from my boardinghouse to the mine. (There was a trolley, but that cost a nickel fare each way, and I was counting my savings by nickels those days.) That accounts for ten hours. It took me another ten of sleep to keep my strength up, for throughout that year I had to train myself like the athlete I had become—and I knew my living depended on my health.

The four hours that were left went for eating, and trying to figure out how to get out of this economic cul-de-sac and on with my life. One way seemed to be to put by enough money so that I could support myself while I looked around. Another was to enlist the assistance of the United States mails.

A cousin in New York had gotten me my job in Grass Valley —through a director of the company that owned the mine—and I had gone down to thank him for it while I was still in college. During a rash moment, he had said, "Let me know what you think of the mine after you get there." It wasn't long before he was hearing, all right—in letters literally thousands of words long, describing every aspect of the operation. I spent one whole letter on labor relations, advocating the institution of an incentive system. I had an axe to grind on that subject.

There is no substitute for the sincerity of a simple heart; that was the letter that did the trick. The cousin couldn't resist passing my letter on to his friend, the director of the company; and the director endorsed it through to the president. It came back through channels, with the latter's penciled note: "Your young man will go far in this company—if his patience with us holds out."

These cryptic words reached my father, and he relayed them to me with the sage advice that I keep my shirt on. It was wasted. He might have saved his breath—or, better still, not forwarded the president's sarcasm. For all I could read of the letter were the first six words, and I took them to be a ringing vote of confidence. Within a week after I got them I had quit my job and was on my way home to plead my case with him personally—for a job as a trained engineer rather than a day laborer.

That wasn't quite all there was to it. Most of my Sundays I had spent trying to write pieces for magazines. The ones I did on life underground came back with monotonous regularity, but a travel piece on that famous flight with Hooker from Paris to

Rome was bought by—of all things—*Vogue,* which published it
as a back-of-the-book filler and paid me forty dollars. The com-
parison of forty dollars for a morning's work with four-fifty for
a whole day's was an inviting one to contemplate.

And besides, while all this had been going on I had come into
money. When Mother had died in 1910, her estate had consisted
of the house I'd been born in in New Haven. Father had put it
in her name; she left it to my sisters and me. After Father had sold
it for us and paid some expenses, there was still five thousand
dollars' worth of securities on the New York Stock Exchange for
my share. These became my uncontested property at 12:01 on the
morning of my birthday, December 8, 1921.

There was also, in 1921, the Great Dream from which the
whole Ingersoll family was yet to awaken. The Great Dream was
Aunt Emily, a maiden lady with—who knew how much money
she might leave to us?

All families should—and a lot of families do—have an Aunt
Emily in the background while they're growing up. It makes for
self-confidence, and it is such a comfort.

Our Aunt Emily was already in her seventies when I was a boy,
and she lived in a small frame house in White Plains with twenty
or thirty cats, a dozen or more parrots, two female "companions,"
and a Rolls-Royce. The fascinating fact about the Rolls was that
it could be driven only over a very few miles of pavement in the
immediate vicinity of her house. To make it easy to get in and out
of it, she had had the frame so altered that its clearance amid-
ships was a scant six inches. This made it impossible for the car
to surmount even the most modest obstacle. But that didn't bother
Aunt Emily, because she only went out in it on the very few days
of each year that the temperature and the humidity outdoors
suited her.

Other times, Aunt Emily remained in residence with her parrots
and her cats, and received annual calls from the Ingersoll family.
We were her closest relatives.

Aunt Em's money had come down from old Zadoc Pratt, whose only son—the one who'd been killed in the Battle of Bull Run —had married a relative of hers. No one had any idea how much money there was, for Aunt Emily had left everything in the hands of the old Fifth Avenue Bank, which had been her father's, and the Fifth Avenue Bank wouldn't talk. But even with two companions and a chauffeur to support, it was suspected that Aunt Emily couldn't possibly be spending the income on a fortune that might have been half a million dollars when she was a girl.

Almost the first thing that happened to me when I got back from Grass Valley was a command visit to Aunt Emily, whom I hadn't seen in half a dozen years. It was my sisters, not I, who had nourished great expectations; in my teens I considered their speculations on Aunt Emily's death indecent. But now I admitted to being curious, and my father and Tante and I took a train out to White Plains one Sunday afternoon to visit with her.

I had only the vaguest memories of Aunt Emily's hardwood castle—everything, even the furniture, seemed to be made of oak, glossed up and shined to within an inch of its life. However, nothing seemed to have changed except Aunt Emily. I'd remembered her as a frail old lady who pottered about but was quite lively and responsive. Now, in her eighties, she'd run to flesh in her wheel chair, and it took only a few polite passages to demonstrate that she was far gone in senility. She hadn't the remotest idea who any of us were, try as hard as her two female companions could to explain.

My father was clearly hurt and confused, for he had been Aunt Emily's lifelong intimate, and her adviser on everything but money matters. My own tough-minded thought was, "Well, that's that. Whatever is in Aunt Emily's will is there to stay, for she'll never write another." And I wondered if it really was true that she had a fortune to leave anybody. The second vice-president of a bank could have afforded the house she lived in. I think I was in the act of musing on this subject when the old lady caught my eye and perked up noticeably.

"You're a very large young man," she said, "whoever you are. I have a nephew as big as you. His name is Ralph. He's the only one in the family who amounts to anything; he's out west earning his living with a pick and shovel."

When Aunt Emily died, a few years after this conversation, and they finally got around to opening up her safe-deposit boxes in the Fifth Avenue Bank, they found half a dozen whole issues of once-good securities that were now valueless because their owner had failed to turn them in for new issues or had let them go by some default. But the value of the securities whose rights had *not* expired came to the grand total of twenty-some million dollars! Of such is the miracle of stock dividends and compound interest.

The will that distributed this sizable hunk of spending money had been written years before, on the clear assumption that the total value of the estate might be as much as a single million. Of this, nine hundred thousand went specifically to charitable institutions by name—including, of course, specialists in the welfare of parrots and cats. Also as specific bequests, the odd hundred thousand was divided between my father and his brother. And then, obviously at the prompting of a routine legal question, it was added that if there were any assets left, the residue should go to the survivors of a distant young cousin, male, who had deceased when she was a girl. Father said she must have had a shine on him once.

Half a dozen of these heirs were subsequently located, all living either in Germany or France. And that is the end of the saga of Aunt Emily's millions.

The only effect her death had on my life was to take some of the savor out of my more extravagant daydreams. But how distressing it might have been if any of us had had any idea that she had *that* much money; I am certain that only our ignorance had kept us all as blissfully independent as we were.

But to get back from my daydream to life in Grass Valley: Walking to work to save a nickel was just as important to me the day after I came into the money I did as the day before. Only a New Englander can truly understand this phenomenon—in a naturally extravagant boy. I'd been raised on the assumption that there were two kinds of money in the world, only one of which was common currency. The other was a mystic thing called "capital" and could not ever, under any circumstances, be used except for reinvestment. To spend capital was much worse than unwise or ill advised; it was even worse than simply sinful: it was positive proof of degeneracy. I had been so thoroughly conditioned that, even though I might acknowledge half a dozen other sins as irresistible, the idea of spending capital was so awful that it was beyond even me.

So I couldn't touch the five thousand; but I did accept the fact that the dividends were mine. And these, I recall, added up to a few dollars over three hundred a year: I was now getting almost a dollar a day, for absolutely no effort! The possibilities of life as a Capitalist were opening up rapidly. With the coming of spring, I decided to quit, and did.

I made quite a thing of my journey home when I got around to making it. It would have been too easy to run down on the wood-burning narrow gauge to Truckee, where the transcontinental trains stopped on their way east. That would have got me home in three days. Instead, I decided to take ten and see the world.

For me, this meant revisiting San Francisco and then taking the southern transcontinental route to New Orleans. But the only way I could stretch my savings to cover all this mileage was to take what was then known as a "tourist train." In these early precursors of the Greyhound bus, you rode four to a Pullman section, in cars that were locked off from even the day coaches—and brought your own food for the interminable six-day journey.

The Pullmans assigned to this work were the last of the wooden variety, and the wonder is that they didn't catch fire crossing the desert in the early summer heat. When we went through Needles, the temperature outside was one hundred and twenty. Inside our car, life was enlivened by the fact that four of its occupants were insane military prisoners, shackled together and guarded by a whole squad of soldiers with rifles.

For New Orleans, I had set aside three days and fifty dollars. But by the time we got there, I had had my belly full of travel for travel's sake.

They were announcing the departure of a northbound train from the same station when we pulled into it. A great wave of homesickness seized me; New Orleans could wait. My baggage under my arms, I ran for the northbound express and caught it. My last fifty dollars went for a berth to stretch out in alone and meals first-class in the dining car. Even so, from New Orleans to New York it seemed to me that I counted the clicks of every rail we passed over. All I wanted in the whole wide world was to feel a New York sidewalk under my feet again.

These are the wages of impatience:

Not only had my patron, the president of the company, no job for me now, but I could not even get to see him. Nor would my father even discuss the proposition of a career in literature.

I was in disgrace, and only Arny and my friend Bishop were glad to see me.

Within three months I was back in Grand Central taking yet another train west to yet another mine. Only this time there was no Jeannine to see me off.

XII · Greenwich Village in Brooklyn

On my way east a second time, I was anything but as brave as I had hoped I would be. I had come by my final "final decision" to quit mining without consulting anyone. Naturally, as soon as it was made, I regretted it. In the end, I had been weeks screwing my courage to the sticking point and breaking the news to my boss. And he had taken it so well that all the seams of my doubt were reopened.

The confidence I had had was based on a scant six months' "success" as a genuine mining engineer at last—at $150 a month and room and board—on a Phelps Dodge property a hundred or so miles south of the Mexican border. There I did the work of a division engineer underground, and lived, above, as one of a small colony of congenial expatriates. I had promoted the job myself, after working as a journeyman miner in Bisbee, Arizona.

Theoretically, I should have been very happy, but no sooner was I a single rung up the ladder than I felt climbing the rest of the way would be a purposeless bore. After all, I had now proved I could do it—and that was all that seemed important. That was what Father had required that I prove to him; now I could try something *I* wanted to do. What? The only thing of which I was really sure was that I didn't know.

So once again, but this time for good, I called it "deep enough" —which is a miner's way of saying he's through—and set out for home. And it was then that my courage began to ooze.

It was all very well to be brave making up my own mind for myself, walking alone on a hilltop, with the wind and the sun for reassurance, but I had been so dependent on my father's approval that I had no real confidence that I could live without it, or get it.

So I came east hoping against hope that I could present my decision to find another career so serenely that my father would give me his blessing. But when I arrived at last at Evergreen Farm, in the Berkshire Hills, all my worst fears were realized.

In Father's presence, I lost all the swagger I had acquired as a division engineer in Mexico. We sat under the big maple on the lawn and talked and talked. And the longer we talked, the less convincing I sounded, even to myself—and Father was totally unmoved toward my point of view. His face, which had lines in it now, grew longer and longer, until even his ferocious white mustaches seemed to droop. If he had become angry, my courage might have been rekindled by a spark; but he seemed only depressed and humiliated by this final evidence that he had a fool for a son.

I went sadly away, to entrain for New York, with every vestige of confidence gone. Instead of convincing Father, I had convinced myself: that I was inherently scatterbrained, without judgment or character, without coherent purpose or sense of responsibility. Nor was there anything I could do about it.

I stood forlorn on the station platform at Millerton, New York, and a cheerful young man a few years older than I said hello. I could not remember his name—which turned out to be Charlie Martin—but did recall vaguely having met him. We rode down on the train together, and I found him easy to talk with. When he heard that I was going to New York to look for a job—at I didn't know what—and that I had no place to stay, instead of being sorry for me he thought it was a wonderful joke. He ended by offering me a bed in the cellar of his family's house in Brooklyn Heights. "All it will cost you will be the carfare to get over to Manhattan to look for a job."

Charlie himself lived in the cellar, too, because all but his mother's and sister's rooms (and one other, upstairs) were let to roomers. The romantic fact, then unknown to me, was that Charlie's father (who lived in the other room which was unlet upstairs) had only just been taken back into the family which he had hopelessly ruined a few years earlier.

I never knew the details of the scandal, but he was the live skeleton in the closet, hidden, and never mentioned by his wife. She had taken in the roomers to bring up his children. The Martins, in their way, were as extraordinary a family as the Emmets. They had made a lark of keeping their home and themselves together —and building new lives. They were good medicine for a boy who was sorry for himself. Once prosperous and proud, they had not a single friend left from the days before the disgrace. It was like Charlie to bring home a stray dog like me, and I was cheerfully accepted and assigned a cot across the room from the sink in which Charlie made the family gin.

It was in this strangely secure retreat that I began to recover from the awful consequence of having defied my father—and of being stuck with my defiance. But the way was slow and hard. For a single letter or a telephone call, I am sure I would have gone contritely home—to resign myself to Father's eminent good sense and a career in mining. Far from being reassured that I had done the right thing, I was certain that I was living with myself in sin.

For one thing, I was soon having much too good a time— meeting Charlie's friends and posing fraudulently as one who was giving up all for art. And I was enjoying their company and learning to drink with the best of them. This is the worst kind of evidence with which to reassure a New England conscience.

Moreover, ingenious as I had now become at making a dollar do the work of ten, it couldn't be long before my savings were exhausted—and those sacred inherited securities were now like the last swigs of water at the bottom of the canteen to a man lost in the desert; to have touched them would have been an admission of the End.

But the really horrible thing was that the more thoroughly I proved my worthlessness, the more I enjoyed it! There just wasn't any denying that being a fraud was fun, which made it all just so much more distressing. That was a sad summer for my puritan principles.

When Martin bought me, he bought my friend Bishop, too. We soon became a threesome on the town. But when we weren't enjoying ourselves, the underlying seriousness of their purposes was a final reproach to me. While by now I had abandoned even the pretense of looking for a job, Martin was going to work every day, contributing to his family's support; and Bishop was an all-too-serious medical student. Both were articulately ambitious.

Once, talking together about each other's dreams, it was Charlie's proposal that whoever first achieved the goal of his heart should celebrate by giving a dinner—the best, the most wonderful, and the most expensive dinner in town—for the other two. It seemed a marvelous idea; Bish and I agreed.

The occasion of Bishop's treat was to be his getting his M.D.

—of which he was even less sure, now that he was in medical school, than he had been as an undergraduate. Charlie was a clerk in a bank; he would pay off on the great day when they made him an officer. For want of a better idea, I said I would save up for the day I had a book of mine published. But even with Charlie's cheery encouragement and Bishop's stubborn faith, I was sure I had them in a sucker bet.

It could be this and it could be that—or maybe it was just a dripping away of conscience on the soft foundation of my career as a carefree soul—but there came a day when I could no longer take it. I hadn't written a line since I'd come to New York and did not expect I ever again would. And the next step I took made it even more unlikely that Charlie and Bish would ever celebrate at my expense. The job I wanted was somewhere in the literary world, but I had not a single connection with anyone who might have something to offer. So, like the well-trained young engineer I had been, I made an engineering project of it.

As a candidate for a job handling words instead of shovels, the nearest thing I had to credentials (as even a would-be author) was graduation from Blanche Colton Williams' course at Columbia University's Summer School in short-story writing. That stint had come between adventures in Grass Valley, California, and Bisbee and Nacozari, in Arizona and Mexico. As a writer, I learned little; when, eventually, I became an editor, I found I had learned a lot. In Blanche Williams' then-famous course it was required of each student that he read one story written by each and every other student, in a class that numbered in the hundreds, most of them Midwestern teachers, female. There can be, in my opinion, no better way of housebreaking puppy editors than thus to rub their snotty little noses in every known form of literary cliché. After reading only a few score of the manuscripts poor Blanche had to mark, nausea, at the recognition of an outworn cliché, clumsily used, set in soon, and overpoweringly.

But I could hardly sell myself as a likely employee in the

literary world with only a summer at Columbia to back me up.
So out of the classified telephone book, I copied the names of
every newspaper, magazine, and book-publishing house in New
York. Then I scheduled eight hours a day of calling on their
offices, working with a map of Manhattan to group them. That
was to save time and shoe leather, getting from one to the next.
With such forethought, I figured I could get in at least sixteen
calls a day—which, lots of days, I actually did. I didn't know
what kind of work I would get, but I hadn't the least doubt that
I'd get *something:* it seemed only mathematical probability that
if I kept my calls up long enough, some day at some door they'd
be needing somebody at the exact hour of my arrival.

And so it was that for the next six weeks I made these solemn
rounds—and never, in but a single instance, got past a receptionist. I was all dressed up and had my hair cut and my shoes
shined, the way the book says, but it didn't help. The single
exception was the New York *Tribune*'s office, where, on my third
visit, a city editor named Stanley Walker did me the honor of
looking me over. He was not impressed.

But just the same, it was this routine that paid off. By the sixth
week, I was going around in a kind of daze. I had long left hope
behind and, as if snow-blind in a blizzard, I kept moving only
because if I stopped I felt I would surely perish. I had speaking
acquaintances with every receptionist in the business—and some
of them were very nice to me and even pretended that their
bosses were thinking of seeing me . . . soon.

And then one day it came time for me to do lower Fourth
Avenue again, and I made my usual call on The Century Company, which was then a top-flight book-publishing house. It was
my umpteenth appearance there, and I was surprised to find a
new girl at the switchboard by the swinging gate. I was so surprised, in fact, that instead of asking formally if I could see
Mr. Frank, I just blurted, "Is Glenn Frank in?" as if I were an
old friend. She waved me past.

And there I was, suddenly and wholly unprepared, standing

in the great man's office, and he sitting in his shirt sleeves behind his desk, facing me!

It was a scorcher of an August day, and poor Editor Frank
was busy to distraction. When his only greeting was, "Well, what
do *you* want?" I lost the nerve to ask him for a job. Seeing the
pile of thick manuscripts on the desk before him, I answered
insincerely, "I want to write a book." It seemed more dignified to
say that.

From there on, the dialogue was fast and to the point. To
Frank's "About what?" the only thought that came in my head
was "a mine in Mexico."

"Then why don't you write it?" he barked.

This time I answered truthfully, "I don't know how."

That *really* got him. Half to get rid of me and half in amusement, I expect, he said, "It's really very easy, you know—writing
a book. You just decide how many chapters it is going to have,
and give each one of them a name. Then, under each chapter's
name, you set down what you're going to put in it. Now, that's
your outline. You just go right ahead and write Chapter I."

I was fascinated and said, "And after that?"—upon which the
famous editor closed the conversation by saying, not unkindly
now, "Well, son, when you get that far—well, after you've written the first three or four chapters—oh, bring them in and I'll
tell you whether it's worth your while going on at all."

Poor man; forty-eight hours later I was back with *five* chapters.

I had gone home to Charlie's cellar and hammered them out
on the battered old Remington my father had given me on my
tenth birthday and I had lugged around with me ever since.

My reappearance at The Century Company was almost as unorthodox as my earlier visit. The regular girl was back on the job
and wouldn't let me by for a long time. When I did get through,
I found Mr. Frank as busy as ever and as frankly startled as you
might expect. When I plunked my carefully typed manuscript
on top of the pile in front of him, he should by all rights have
said, "I'll let you know." But I had taken his fortress by storm

now, and he sat meekly back and read the thing there and then. When he had finished, instead of giving me a yes or no, he bolted through an interoffice door, and I was left alone.

"Good God," was my horrified thought. "It's so bad that it has made him ill!"

I really thought that—and was dumbfounded when he returned a few minutes later with another shirt-sleeved executive, saying, "This is So-and-So, our Book Editor. He's got a contract for you to sign—and after you've signed it, will you please get out of here; because I really am busy."

"A contract for what?" I asked.

"For this book, when you finish it."

I was to be an author at last, despite myself!

Glenn Frank and the girl on the switchboard who let me in by mistake aren't the only ones whom I must credit with assists on that first book. There is also Julie to account for.

Julie was the girl I had settled on early in my adventures in Bohemia; and she was in the process of settling for me. A few years older than I, she had been a girl of Charlie's and was still a pal of his, although she had a lot of other beaux. She had a pert little face, a trim figure, and a quick wit that had acid in it. But despite her sharpness, her laughter was gay and unaffected.

Julie was most eminently a girl of her time: the only daughter of an upstate judge, she had wheedled her father into setting her up in a small apartment of her own, just off Greenwich Village. She'd been an English major, *magna cum laude,* at Vassar, and by the time I knew her she was supporting herself as a junior editor on one of the big fashion magazines. She had more talent with words, and was a more perceptive critic, than her job demanded. Julie might well have made her mark in the literary world if things had turned out differently.

Julie and I hit it off from our first date; it seems to me that I took her by extravagant taxi to the Bossert Roof where a breathtaking view of lower Manhattan came free with the table d'hôte.

As an aspirant to sophistication, I made such a good impression that she did me the honor of assuming that my motives were dishonorable. I couldn't have been more flattered than by her pointed insistence that we say good night to each other outside the door to her apartment. So encouraged, it wasn't too long before we didn't—and we found ourselves very happy with our new arrangement. We were very discreet about it, but there was no question but that I had taken Julie out of circulation.

Thereafter we learned about each other and the city we lived in as two young people should, each day planning for the next what might be most fun to do with what funds I could scrape up —from bridge winnings at the Bishops', a six-dollar dividend check, or a handout Arny might have persuaded my father to send me. Life wasn't too expensive those days, when you got red ink with your dollar and a quarter Italian dinner and could sit until dawn in a tiny Russian restaurant nursing the two dollars' worth of drinks that came with the cover charge. And there were always open-topped two-decker buses to ride upon, or open trolley cars on Lexington Avenue. One's gin one made oneself, and drank with orange juice. For a Big Binge, there were occasional public balls—usually impromptu fancy dress—in Webster Hall or some Village place. (Mostly Julie and I considered the Village beneath us—kid stuff or, at best, touristy.) Also there were the cocktail parties our friends gave uptown; sometimes we went to them, but more often not; I was as jealous of Julie's reputation as she.

It could have been the implied reproach of Julie's going to work each weekday that first revived my own interest in getting a job. I don't remember the exact sequence. But when Century agreed to take my book, my relations with Julie took a new turn. Without invitation, she became my schoolmistress as well as my girl. I had written my sample chapters without consulting her because I was shy about them. But now every word I wrote got Julie's savage professional criticism, for in her *magna-cum-laude* book I was an ignoramus. To pencil-editing my copy, she soon added her own course in required reading, and it was from Julie that I learned about Flandrau and Douglas and such.

One result was that I moved my working quarters over from Charlie's basement to Julie's living room. Since for propriety's sake I was usually put out around midnight with the cat, I'd come prancing back each morning in time to see her off to work, and then sit down to my typewriter in her empty rooms to do my stint. I always felt like a housewife, tidying up the place each afternoon in time for Julie's return, tired out from a hard day at the office. It was then that I'd have her Orange Blossom ready and chilled, and her warm bath drawn. If I'd known how, I would have laid out a change of clothing for her—I was that close to the makings of a perfect houseman.

And so the Book was finally done, and turned in, punctuation perfect—and the proofs read when they came back.

And what a wonderfully glorious day it was when the first bound copies arrived, fresh from the presses, shiny new, done! By that time I felt it was as much her book as mine.

So Julie got herself kissed as she'd never been kissed before. Or maybe it was me who got *himself* kissed. Anyway, we couldn't have been happier.

XIII · The Sands Run Out

The sands of my childhood were running out rapidly now.

The book The Century Company had so bravely commissioned was called *In and Under Mexico,* and because a good house had published it, it was respectfully reviewed. The critic on the *Tribune,* which was the paper I had most wanted to get on, even commented that he thought I had a future as a writer—"if I did not sell my birthright for a mess of pottage," he added gratuitously. But as far as I was concerned, as soon as I got everything I knew about life in a mining camp on paper, I didn't have anything left to write about.

And it was not too long after the book's publication that I began to learn the facts of a literary life. From first word written to first copy sold, *In and Under Mexico* had used up a year of my life; its earnings, as I remember them, were somewhere between one thousand and fifteen hundred dollars. As the author of a book that had been authentically published and well reviewed, I was now almost a respectable member of Manhattan's Bohemia; but all *that* got me was a few more invitations to cocktail parties. No great mental effort was required to forecast what would become of me if I rested on such meager laurels; I had still to find that job.

Other things were happening to me, too, to prove that life was grim and that I had better start being earnest. Julie was becoming restless, less content with me as a gay cavalier—or with herself as a bachelor girl who was asked to parties for her wit, and resented when she got there because she was still single. The Married Women's Union, which has a local in Bohemia, too, was putting on the heat for her to join up.

I was peculiarly dense about this because the relationship Julie and I had seemed to me ideal. *I* was happy, and what more could a girl want than her freedom from convention? If she needed a man, I was always available—and faithful, too, and appreciative; yet, in addition to me, she had also her right to an absolute privacy. I greatly envied Julie her snug little flat, hidden away in the West Twenties, from which she could shut out the world when she chose.

Once, in college, I had written a piece advancing the thesis that the human being most to be envied was a beautiful woman unhandicapped by morality, yet with wit enough to stay unattached. The world was at her feet. It would remain there as long as her looks held out. And after that—well, who wanted to live forever? Or *then* she could get married and sell her independence for security.

Julie was not *that* good looking, but her life was a working approximation of what I had had in mind. If she had cared for richer beaux than I, she could have had them, complete with perquisites; males were always buzzing around her. But instead of being contented with this state of affairs, Julie was now talking more and more resentfully of the limitations imposed by being unwed. Clearly, she was a bourgeois at heart!

Finally, one day when we were riding in a train on the way back from a visit to her family—she had asked me to go along to keep her company—Julie popped the question. "I want to get married," she said abruptly. "I want you to marry me." That suddenly the dream was over and the lights went on.

Julie was very dear to me, and I could feel the hurt in her for having to ask of me what she must so long have wanted me to ask of her. So I said no, at once and not hesitating, to end it cleanly.

Julie cried the rest of the way to New York, and I felt terrible but knew that I had no other choice. I was much too fond of Julie to saddle her with me, knowing that I would never be in love with her the way I had been—and probably still was—in love with Constance. But for the memory of loving Constance, I would have been glad to marry Julie, who had so many things about her that I admired, and with whom I had been so happy.

After the train ride, it was never again the same between Julie and me; all I could do for her after that was to help her get back into circulation. A year or two later, she married a very decent sort of fellow to whom she was very faithful; she made him an excellent wife.

So once again I was up against reality, and the necessity of getting on with life. I was lonely and I was scared; but I was learning. I was finding out the hard way that there are price tags attached to living your life the way you want to live it—and not the way other people think you ought. Whether my motives in being so independent were idealistic or simply hog-selfish, I would not know even now, but the point at which I began to realize that I had consequences to face I consider the conclusion of my childhood.

As so often in my life, it was luck that ended the first of my dilemmas: the job I had been trying to find for a year came and sat next to me at a dinner I had attended only out of politeness. The dinner was one of Aunt Charlotte Bishop's heavier affairs, and the job—as a reporter on a metropolitan paper—came in the person of a Hearst executive who happened to be a fellow guest. When I asked him if he could get me an interview with one of his editors, his answer was, "If you really want to work, I'll put you on myself." This he did. A telegram confirming the job arrived on my doorstep the next morning. After all the shoe leather I had worn out, in the end it was that way.

The job was as a cub reporter on the now-defunct *Morning American*—at twenty-two dollars and fifty cents a six-day, sixteen-hour-a-day, week. I decided that I had found my calling.

But even before that day—it was April 30, 1923—I had passed the real test of manhood: my father's acknowledgment that I was grown. It was a sad and an embarrassing business for me, and I was wholly unprepared for it.

From the day of Father's final discouragement with me, I had more often than not agreed with his opinion of me as a fool. If he had been perceptive enough to put it "a foolish *child*," I could have looked forward to the day I would be grown. But neither of us thought of me then as immature, so that my self-evident foolishness was accepted by both of us not only as inherent but also as permanent. It was my *character* that was at fault. Since I still vastly respected him, and honored his judgment even though I could not follow it, it was therefore the severest of shocks when I woke up one morning to find his opinion of me wholly changed.

The very traits he had most criticized in me, he now admired: my reliance on my own judgment, my "idealism" (in not resigning myself to a career I thought "second best"), and—of all things—my perseverance! By my stubbornness about having my own way, I had proved my "stick-to-itiveness." And the thing of which he was suddenly proudest was the way in which I had stood up to him, defied his threat of disinheritance and challenged his will with my own—the very same behavior that had once hurt him most.

And all it had taken to effect this dramatic about-face had been the publication of a wretched little book with an awkward title and my name on its ugly cardboard cover. I couldn't have been happier about its publication, but I was certainly under no illusion that *In and Under Mexico* was literature—and I was anything but sure that I could ever write another even as good as that. As a literary discovery, I knew *I* was a fraud; and so my father seemed suddenly revealed as a fraud himself.

From an august symbol of righteous wisdom he was suddenly shrunk to the dimensions of a mortal; he was not a god after all, but simply a nice old gentleman gone silly about his son.

The whole experience was of disenchantment, and it took me many years to get over it and to reappraise my father at his true worth. When I was twenty-three, Father's lack of literary judgment depressed me, for literary judgment was the only kind of judgment I then acknowledged. But that wasn't the shocking part of the business. It was the crumbling of his fortifications as a man, his surrender to his son's will without giving further battle. I had licked him too easily. I was ashamed for both of us.

Father remained in a kind of trance about me for the rest of his long, long life. Even the most appalling of scrapes I got into, he forgave and tried hard to understand. I could marry women he did not like, vote for Presidents he abhorred—and even lose all my money gambling in the stock market on margin—but still he was for me and against any detractor. Eventually I got over my embarrassment and came to love him very dearly.

The summer in which I grew up was the summer before my twenty-third birthday. That was during the year before I met my first murderer and punched my first city editor in the nose—and I didn't even know Harold Ross's name, or that a magazine he was even then inventing would be my first true love.

Part II

XIV · A Man Named Harold Ross

To show you how complicated my feelings about Harold Ross became, in 1935 I wrote (and published) thirty-five thousand words on the subject of his magazine—and never even mentioned the fact that I had been its managing editor for five years.

During those five years—which ran from 1925 to 1930—I had thought *The New Yorker* as much my property as Ross's. This in itself was peculiar, because I would have fought physically at the slightest suggestion that Ross was not the sole proprietor of his idea for a sophisticated magazine about New York. It was simply that my identification with the undertaking was that complete. It was truly as if the magazine was my only family, and I passionately dedicated to its survival. And Ross was the total father image—the creator of this family which was now *mine*. As the creator, he could be idolized and imitated, ridiculed or savagely criticized—but he had always to be defended.

The magazine in which I published my thirty-five-thousand-word history of Harold W. Ross's journal was *Fortune*. I had left the home in which I'd grown up as a journalist, as it were, to manage *Fortune* for Henry Robinson Luce. Since the article itself was both a defiance and a desperate effort to achieve a proper perspective, my decision was to keep it pure by omitting any reference to myself. Then not even Ross could laugh at however I might describe my own role in *The New Yorker*'s success, because there wouldn't be any description of it at all. And—ten cents on the side—the only world I respected knew exactly what I had (and hadn't) done anyway.

What I had done, for the record, was to let Ross talk himself into hiring me as a reporter on June 13, 1925, four months after Vol. I, No. 1. So violent was the turnover in those days that within five more months I was Ross's senior editorial employee and, titularly, his Managing Editor.

This titular managing editorship had been conferred with demoniac glee—to fill a vacant line in the owners' statement which is required to be published every six months by the Post Office Department. And Ross took personal pleasure in informing me that I was just about as qualified to be anybody's managing editor as Carmen. Carmen was our office boy.

Actually, my job that summer had been to put together *The New Yorker*'s "Talk of the Town" department, a kind of miniature magazine within a magazine, which, just before I came, had been written by a former sports-writer named James Kelvin McGinnis and for some obscure reason signed Van Bibber III. "The Talk of the Town" was my only creative contribution to *The New*

Yorker's formula, and for practical purposes I had finished that contribution in my first six months there. It was never improved on, and I consider the present-day "Talk" a sloppy job of work.

I was responsible for the "Talk of the Town" for as long as I was with *The New Yorker,* but soon had many other duties as well. Ross had hardly got through laughing at the idea of my being a managing editor when, for want of something nearer the mark, he began using me as one.

Lest there are professionals in the audience, I hasten to add a qualification. It is the normal full-time routine of a managing editor to manage—to hire and fire and assign, to schedule, and to see that the publication gets to press on time. In the Ross version, the managing part was a side line to be accomplished in coffee breaks or while Ross was on the telephone trying to explain himself to whichever contributor he had most recently insulted. The main part of the job was to listen to and argue with Ross himself, hour after precious hour while one's desk piled higher with chores that had to be done despite him in order to get the magazine out at all.

The urgency of Ross's need for a whipping boy to argue with was so great that mealtimes were not excepted; there was once a period of nearly a year when I rarely ate less than two meals a day with Ross and often three, sometimes being called to his house before breakfast, while he was still shaving.

In *The New Yorker*'s early days, the blessed—or cursed—individual who found himself in this intimate working relationship with Ross was known locally as a "Jesus." However the Post Office wanted it put, the record is that I was *The New Yorker*'s first Jesus. A Jesus, of course, must eventually be crucified, and after a while I was. But for a long time I held the record tenure of office, being Ross's creature for a matter of years. And unlike a number of my successors, I survived to remain a senior executive. After all, when Ross began appointing Jesuses from outside the organization, *someone* had to get the magazine to press. But by that time things had shaken down to where I was responsible for the nonfiction features and Katharine White for the literary body—the casuals and profiles. And to the Post Office, we were co-M.E.'s.

I am also to be distinguished from Ross's other Jesuses by the fact that for a giddy month or two I played the role of Ross himself. It took a combination of circumstances to achieve this. My opposite number, *The New Yorker*'s literary editor, was on vacation abroad when an infected wisdom tooth stopped Ross in his tracks, sent him to a hospital, and very nearly killed him.

This was in 1926, during the dramatic period in *The New Yorker*'s career when it was first breaking through into recognition. It had almost—but not quite—been put over. That is, its circulation had been going up for seven or eight months, and the best stores in New York were beginning to advertise in it; but it was still running heavily in the red.

Overnight I was in sole charge, inheriting—and almost permanently—*The New Yorker* tradition that its Editor, not its Publisher or his Business Manager, was the Boss. This dramatic responsibility I handled by lengthening my working day from sixteen to twenty and sometimes twenty-two hours—literally—and going on a diet of coffee, tomato juice, and gin. These seemed to be the only substances I could digest and still work at the pace I was setting myself and everybody else. On it, I got skinnier than I had been as a mucker underground. But my body held out all right—until the week after Ross got back from the hospital. Then I had myself a nervous breakdown the likes of which I never want to come near again. Its first—and gentlest—symptom was a conviction that I had no legs below the knees, even though I could see and pinch them.

My agony lasted about thirty days. I cured myself, without benefit of psychiatrists, by retiring to my father's farm. There I chopped wood until I was so physically exhausted that I had to fall down and go to sleep—nightmares or no nightmares. While I chopped—cord after cord after cord—the only comfort I found was in chanting to myself, "I don't *ever* have to go back. I don't *ever* have to go back. I don't *ever* have to go back." But I got over that.

Along about the third week I managed my first dreamless sleep, and after that I mended fast. When I thought I could make sense again, I took the train down to New York and walked in on Ross. His only comment was, "Well . . . glad you're back."

"I'm back," I told him, "but I'm darned if I know whether I'm the same guy who left here." So I made him this condition: If he wanted me to stay, he would have to cut my salary until I found out. I didn't want the burden of his expecting more than I knew I could deliver.

After I'd been back about six weeks I went to him again and said, "I'm not merely as good as I was; I'm better. I'll take back my salary and a raise." I got my salary back, but Ross didn't give me the raise for another few months. He was very grudging about raises in those days. He was grudging about salaries in general, in fact: I was his highest-paid editorial executive, and I think what I got was one hundred and fifty a week.

I am now a long way ahead of myself—not unintentionally, I admit, because I wanted to get rid of my own role on *The New Yorker* before I went back to talk about either the magazine's beginnings or the effects on me of all these experiences as I remember them.

I understand that today *The New Yorker* has a circulation of 415,000, sells twelve million dollars' worth of advertising a year, and that the stock in the F-R Company, which publishes it, is traded over the counter on a basis that values the enterprise at better than twelve millions of dollars.

This is a lot of money for a small-town magazine. According to the rules, when Harold W. Ross died in 1951, at least half of it could easily have been his. Not only had the magazine been his idea (and the first twenty thousand it spent, the sum total of his wealth), but for twenty-six years he had been its chief executive and its alter ego. He was as furiously anxious to improve it the day before he died as the day the first issue appeared, on Thursday, February 19, 1925. Yet one of the oddest facts about Ross is that he died without a share of the stock in his possession.

This was not because he was either luckless or had been defrauded—the man who backed him had been the most generous of capitalists—but for reasons of his own peculiar principles. In the beginning, Ross had grudgingly accepted a modest ten per cent. Gradually, as *The New Yorker* grew rich and successful, he sold even this for the stated reason that to have a financial interest in his own venture compromised him. He could not function happily as the master in his own house if his judgment was corrupted by a financial self-interest.

By an odd circumstance, it was through me that Ross disposed of the last of his stock. I bought it for the Time, Inc. organization as an investment, some time in the middle thirties. (We made a profit selling it back to his associates, who would have been glad to have bought it in the first place had Ross cared to offer it to them.) That was the kind of man Ross was—that pure and that peculiar.

Although he was born in Aspen, Colorado, Utah was where the Ross story really began. Harold's father was not a Mormon. But his uncle joined the church to get trade for his Salt Lake City grocery store. When Harold was fourteen he used to work in this store, and before he became sensitive about his eccentricities he would talk about his career there. He used to explain that he was so explosive a practical joker that his uncle once remarked no matter how well a business was founded, Harold could wreck it in two weeks. So just before the two weeks were up, he was fired. Long before *The New Yorker* was a success, its principal owner, Raoul Fleischmann, could sympathize with Ross's uncle.

Few individuals were more fascinating to caricature than Ross. His face was made of rubber, which stretched in every direction. Out of the lower half hung a huge Hapsburg lip to which cigarettes stuck. Widespread teeth diverged downward, and ramrod-straight hair rose up from his forehead, diverging upward and outward. It was Ina Claire who first remarked that her life's ambition was to walk through it barefoot.

Under heavy eyebrows, Ross's eyes were fierce, shifty, and restless. He was nervous beyond belief. Wildly, with great sweeping gestures, he talked—with furious intensity, with steady unimaginative profanity. And in a sudden alternation of mood, he could seem as shy and moody as a child. He had charm, and the vitality of a mad bull.

This strange Lochinvar came out of the West with his legend already abuilding, even when he was still in his teens. His journalistic career began in his native Salt Lake City, where he had disclaimed interest in the parental Ross Wrecking Company—a business then described as "materials reclaiming." He went to work as an office boy on a Salt Lake paper, still a kid in military school, who stripped off his uniform coat after classes and ran errands for the editor in the militia's pants.

Ross was only eighteen when he pulled out of Salt Lake City. He never went to college, and for the next seven years he drifted, a vagabond reporter. When I first knew him he was best remembered around the Golden Gate—he was the waterfront man for the San Francisco *Call*—for his success in providing the local newspaper club with an elegant free set of wicker furniture. The club being a little short of funds, Ross had pinched a police launch, sneaked out to the Panama Pacific Exposition grounds facing Golden Gate, leaped ashore, and cabbaged all the furniture from the about-to-be-dismantled Danish building. His most famous friend in San Francisco was the then Crown Prince of Siam, whom he once chaperoned on a see-night-life-incognito tour. And his local nickname was "Rough House."

But it was in Atlanta that Ross's reputation as a reporter was made, when he covered the Franks rape and lynching. There he was known as the greatest picture swiper ever to operate in Georgia. Competing with a Hearst paper, he was so good he could reswipe the pictures the Hearst reporters had already swiped from him.

After Atlanta, Ross wandered far afield, almost quit journalism. For a while he bossed a gang of Negroes in Panama. It was the war that brought him back in the fold—and made him.

He enlisted in the Railway Engineers Corps. When his regiment reached Bordeaux, he heard of an army newspaper about to be launched in Paris. It was to be World War I's famous *Stars and Stripes,* and his resolution was to get on its staff. When early inquiries informed him that to do this he must become an officer, he took the military seriously for the first time, worked earnestly as a company clerk, and was rewarded with being chosen one of four enlisted men picked to attend the special officers' school at Langres.

There Ross spent an unhappy winter wading in mud and waiting for his papers, only to learn in the spring that, far from insuring his transfer, his energy had made it impossible. Line officers could not be spared for typewriter pounding. Wild with rage, Ross plunged into the task of getting himself demoted. He overslept conscientiously, left puttees unfastened and his blouse unbuttoned, began talking back to officers. At last he succeeded; he was sent back to Bordeaux a private once more—in disgrace.

But for a second time Ross had outdone himself. So infuriated were his superiors that they exiled him to outpost duty with an old army sergeant and ignored the requests for his transfer that were at last coming through from Paris. His one-time boast was that he found this out by stealing one from a mail pouch. And in the end he had to resort to what he might have done long before. He simply stepped out a window one night and beat his way, A.W.O.L., to Paris.

When helpful friends finally succeeded in setting his papers in order, Ross's ambition was fulfilled at last and he found himself the junior member of the service weekly that was to collect the adventurous cream of contemporary journalism. There were

Alexander Woollcott, Franklin P. Adams, Grantland Rice, and many others.

The stories of those days were once very dear to Ross; he used to tell several different versions of his success in Paris. I never quite believed any of them, but one had it that he had been made editor only because his more famous contemporaries all wanted to get to the front. Ross's appointment was to have been temporary until they could get back to choose his successor. But once he was their boss, he boasted, none of them ever saw Paris again until the war was over. It was his right to order them to wherever he wished.

The *Stars and Stripes*—without advertising or circulation problems—was a far cry from the weekly that Ross eventually created, but there were points of similarity. The *Stars and Stripes* was supposed to be written without benefit of propaganda. Spiritually, it was in revolt against the bombast and hypocritical hoopla of the times. This was the beginning in Europe of the disillusion that characterized the twenties in America when the A.E.F. came home. And Ross was at the heart of it. He had begun to find his dedication—to an honesty in a journalism that was independent of rank or popular hysteria.

A private to the end, Ross had done his job with generals to the right, left, fore, and aft of him. He had run his paper for its audience, made an honest medium in a world short on intellectual honesty. In so doing, he had won the respect of the best journalists of his time. He was now ready for his entrance into New York.

It was not conspicuous. There was an abortive attempt to carry on the *Stars and Stripes,* spirit, staff, and circulation, as *The Home Sector*. Then Ross tried *The American Legion Weekly,* but quit in a huff when he saw it heading into politics. The first humorous magazine he edited was *Judge*—but he made a stormy exit from that one, too, when the owners cut his editorial budget. Disgusted with owners in general now, he turned down fat offers to work on Hearst's *Cosmopolitan* and to edit *Redbook*.

For all this time, beneath the shaving-brush hair, an idea was sprouting—that to get what he wanted he would have to create a weekly of his own. But since this was an idea that needed money to back it, the most important thing that Harold Ross did was to play poker with the Thanatopsis Literary and Inside Straight Club.

F.P.A.'s (Franklin P. Adams's) column in the old New York *World* first made the postwar world conscious of that little group of serious wits who lunched at a round table set aside for them in the Algonquin Hotel. Years later, the proprietor's daughter, Margaret Case, was to write a book about them, but long before that they'd become an integral part of the legend of the Roaring Twenties. Playwrights Marc Connelly and George Kaufman, press agent and *Post* writer John Peter Touhy, the late Alexander Woollcott, Dorothy Parker—the cream of Broadway's literary set were there.

In the early days, most members of the Thanatopsis met Saturday nights in one another's homes to play cards. Again the *Stars and Stripes* motif appears, for the Thanatopsis first met in wartime Nini's in Paris. It was Ross himself who prompted the resurrection in Manhattan, and it was across a round green poker table that he first met Raoul Fleischmann, one of the few outsiders (nonjournalists and nonwriters) to be elected to the group. Their meeting was the real beginning of *The New Yorker*—for all Ross's friends had to offer him by way of encouragement was talk; Fleischmann had money.

xv · Battle in William Street...
and Other Encounters

By the time the Fleischmann family had descended to Raoul it had split in fifteen or twenty directions, accumulating second- and even third-generation millionaires. Originally there were five brothers, Charles, Max, Louis, Henry, and Gustav. Charles and Max were the two who came from Vienna in the early 1870's to start their yeast business in this country. To advertise it they opened a Vienna Bakery at the Philadelphia Centennial in 1876.

It was such a success that after the fair they moved it intact to Broadway at Tenth Street in New York, and put their younger brother Louis in charge of it. Raoul was Louis' youngest son.

It was a charitable idea which Louis thought up that put the word "bread line" in the dictionary. To publicize the fact that Fleischmann bread was fresh bread—and because he was a kindly gentleman—all that was not sold each day was given to the poor each night at 11:00 P.M. Raoul, too, is a kindly gentleman.

When Harold Ross met him playing poker, it was 1924, and Raoul Fleischmann was still dabbling at his father's baking business, managing an uptown branch. He had inherited not quite a million dollars' worth of family stock, but didn't like either yeast or baking. Besides, his new friends of the Algonquin fascinated him, and he enjoyed gambling with them. So Harold Ross had to seek out his office in the baking plant only twice and the thing was done. Ross put up the twenty thousand dollars that was *his* inheritance, and savings from the war years, and Raoul committed himself to go in for at least seventy thousand more. Ross was sure the bill shouldn't be much over a hundred thousand.

It was about this time that I first met Ross—in Katie and Sigmund Spaeth's apartment on the top floor of the old brownstone that housed the Fifth Avenue Bank at Forty- fourth Street and Fifth Avenue. Sigmund played and sold pianos and was soon to become an early radio celebrity as the "Tune Detective"; Katie was Katie: bathtub-gin hostess, blond, theatrical, witty, with a warm heart, a gay lilt to her voice, and talent only for talking. Her place was a kind of early Volstead-era salon where the people she liked or respected dropped in ("dropped in," nonsense . . . climbed three steep flights of stairs!) to "make with words," as Katie might have put it, and Orange Blossoms. She was partial to people who made with words: young playwrights, columnists, press agents, other talkers like herself. Most of them would soon be better known as the Algonquin set; the Algonquin itself was only a block away, on Forty-fourth at Sixth.

The Algonquinite's game was seeking something to say worth either print or quotation. Most Algonquinites played it with such grim intensity that their cruelty to each other, or to such innocents as might cross their path, shocked me. Katie's crowd was my first introduction to the world of wit; it first intrigued and then appalled me.

Ross was in good standing with this group, but more for his explosive appreciation of others' than for his own sallies. He was still shy in the presence of his heroes; actually, his was a deep shyness which, for all his sometimes brashness, he never outgrew. I was on the shy side, too, and I don't remember that Ross and I had much to say to each other at Katie's. But I did know that he was putting together a new magazine on which there would be jobs. Katie even spoke to Ross about me and relayed an invitation to go talk to him.

But I was in a dreamy kind of mood, and had just begun to try to write a novel.

A lot had happened—a lot for those days—since *In and Under Mexico* and Julie.

To begin with, there had been the New York *American*—that job as a reporter that I'd finally gotten at Aunt Charlotte's dinner party. It had been a miniature career in itself, beginning with such sensational success that within weeks I was averaging a column a day in print; and ending, less than six months later, when I did my City Editor the honor of punching him in the nose—and would have beaten up the Managing Editor, too, if he hadn't been tipped off and fled the building.

All this terminal violence was over an elaborate hoax by which my innocence had been taken advantage of—to get a story ordered by The Chief himself, William Randolph Hearst the Elder, then in San Simeon, California. This experience—with the kind of early American journalism that Ben Hecht immortalized in *Front Page*—made as lasting an impression on me as you would expect.

It began (without my knowing it) when a Hearst campaign against the administration of World War I's Veterans Bureau was stalled for lack of new material to keep the story alive. Mud-spattered and smeared beyond recognition, the Bureau had understandably barred its doors to Hearst reporters. Somehow, some way, somebody had to be smuggled back in to get new facts to distort, lest the project die of malnutrition. It was at this juncture that Martin Dunn, the eventually luckless City Editor, thought of me.

I was easy to think of. In the weird and wonderful world of Hearst early-century journalism I was a "Park Avenue Playboy Playing Reporter." This was because my name was in the social register and because I came to work—it was winter—in one of Poly Hooker's cast-off coonskin coats. And I would work six to seven sixteen-hour days a week for twenty-two dollars and fifty cents, no overtime and even carfare begrudged; so I must be rich. I was already kind of a character, noted for being ingenious, aggressive, persistent, and persuasive—and unbelievably (for William Street) unworldly and naïve. For Martin Dunn's present purpose, I was too good to be true, so definitely too good that he decided not to risk stubbing his toe on some silly scruple I might have picked up in my childhood.

So the first I heard of the business was when I was called to his desk and shown (and shown only) a letter signed by Hearst himself. The gist of it was that the *American*'s campaign against the Veterans Bureau had all been a terrible mistake. Honest men and sound principles had suffered for an error in Hearst's own judgment. He wished now to make amends. Would Mr. Dunn therefore assign his "best man" to the preparation of a series of *constructive* articles on the subject. Spare no expense.

I never did find out whether the letter was a whole-cloth forgery or actually had come from San Simeon—but I fell for it, hook, line, and sinker. And my, what a success—from the paper's point of view—it turned out to be!

Irresistibly sincere, I took the poor Veterans Bureau by storm. I gave its bewildered executives "my personal word" that they would be fairly treated, and came back to William Street with the Works—dozens of interviews, whole files of facts, and photographs of everyone concerned. I dumped them all on Martin Dunn's desk, exulting. He had allowed me a month; I had been away a scant two weeks.

The denouement came rapidly. An embarrassed Dunn scooped up the lot and graciously advised me to take a well-earned holiday "before writing the story." It was 11:00 A.M., and the staff of the *Morning American* were just filtering in to work. On my way out of the building, I ran into a fellow reporter whom I had not seen in a month. "What's with you?" I asked. "Oh, I've been out West," he answered, "digging dirt for The Old Man's peeve on the Veterans Bureau"—and he was gone.

The momentum of my happy daze carried me all the way uptown before the significance of these few words began to sink in. And even then I couldn't believe my own horrid suspicions. Not really. I wandered around all day with them, not knowing what to do next. And then, at 6:00 P.M., I got the first bulldog edition at a newsstand!

It hadn't taken Dunn long to act on his windfall. Between 11:00 A.M. and his afternoon deadline he had had my notes rewritten into a scurrilous "exposé of shocking conditions at the V.B."—profusely illustrated with photographs of the men who had given me their confidence, the photographs I had had taken and brought back.

Poor Martin Dunn! He was rather a fatherly man, as I remember him, graying at the temples; and I think he wore glasses to read by. He'd been a kindly tutor my first months in his shop. And now I came thundering across his city room just as he was getting the second edition off to press, past the rewrite men pecking away at new leads, around the horseshoe where

the copyreaders crouched under their green eyeshades. I bore
down on him sitting behind the two-sided city desk with its neat
litter of clippings and scribbled copy paper. I was in the fullest
of regalia, complete with unbuttoned coonskin coat flapping wide
in the breeze and a slouch hat on the back of my head.

On my way across the room, I can remember that my wildly
swinging arms had struck half a dozen shaded light bulbs hanging
by cords from the ceiling and that they were swinging hysterically
in my wake. I paused just long enough to tower over Mr. Dunn
while I got my breath. He was a brave man. He looked up and
said calmly, "Well, what do you want to do about it? Fight a
duel?" I said, "Mr. Dunn, you couldn't be more right," and
sent him crashing backward, swivel chair and all, upsetting the
huge wastebasket that is the city editor's symbol of office. And my
own momentum had me on top of him in a wild snowstorm of
raw material for the second edition.

Someone from the copy desk got me back on my feet, and
with Dunn still sitting in the ruins of his edition I roared,
"Where's that son of a bitch Watson?" and went to find *him*.
Watson was that month's managing editor of the *American*. The
paper was on the downgrade then, and Hearst changed managing
editors every few weeks; but I knew Watson must have been
in on it.

That's about all of the story. The photographer who had
worked with me was a young girl named Helen Kanaga. I never
saw her after the incident, but I understand she later made a
reputation for herself as an art photographer in San Francisco.
That day I met her in the hall, en route to Watson's hastily emp-
tied office, and found her in as white a rage as I. It was her
inspiration to drop in on the darkroom and break every plate
we could yank out of the shelves—they used a lot of plates those
days, when every picture was retouched.

For a giddy half-hour, Kanaga and I owned the shop, and
no one dared approach us. Then, arm in arm, we sallied forth
and celebrated at a speak-easy. Our relations with the New York

American being already far beyond the formality of resignation, neither of us ever went back. But within the month I had been sought out by almost every single reporter on the *American* staff to be congratulated, and told of some similar chicanery of which he or she had been the victim.

To each of these stories there was the same depressing end: "Boy, how I'd like to have done what you did—but what do you do when you have a wife and kids" (or a mother or a sick relative) "to support? You just take it . . . and go buy yourself another drink."

That was the way it was in the early twenties in the Hearst organization. It was never like that on the New York *Times,* though on most other papers the old rough-and-tumble anything-goes-to-get-the-story-the-boss-wants was still the tradition.

Ross never admired me much for my handling of the Hearst incident—years later when he heard about it from me. For all his early nickname of "Rough House," he was terrified of physical violence. Also, he might well have felt that in my innocence I was fair game; he did not consider innocence a virtue, innocent as he himself was in lots of ways. But he felt the same way I did about Hearst, particularly Hearst's corruption of men of talent, his practice of hiring them away from honest employers and then breaking their integrity by the demands he made of them.

Ross felt that Hearst was an evil influence, but his deepest scorn, I think, was reserved for proprietors like Frank Munsey, the tycoon who made his money in groceries and then bought and ran newspapers as if they were grocery stores. At least Hearst was a journalist himself, and an able one. Munsey's only contribution to his time was to cut reporters' salaries to the level of his chain-store clerks'. Ross felt so strongly about this that when Munsey died he published a posthumous attack in the form of an obituary, a "Reporter at Large" piece by Morris Markey. The date was January 2, 1926.

The New York *American* was only the first of several adventures that befell me in my last pre-Rossian years. The battle of the city room might have made me a hero to my confreres, but I doubted if it would help me get another job on a newspaper for a while. And financial backlogs are not accumulated on twenty-two fifty a week so I tried my hand at pulp writing, successfully establishing myself as the anonymous author of an impressive series entitled *Confessions of a Debutante*. The only trouble was that the magazine I wrote them for went broke, and my total take was the forty dollars I got for the first piece.

I had to find some way to keep alive; and something to write about, too. So come spring, I solved both problems temporarily by signing on as a steward's yeoman on the old Munson Line's S.S. *Southern Cross*. It ran between Hoboken and Buenos Aires.

A steward's yeoman's is a pretty good job in the merchant marine. Mine came with a typewriter and a tiny office of its own—and a berth in a third-class cabin with the ship's barber. On the typewriter, I typed menus and manifests; and on the telephone in the office I took calls from passengers requiring the service of bellboys. Passengers' requirements of bellboys, I may say, are of the widest variety and are far from being without interest to a young writer. Since the bellboys themselves were mostly handsome young college students working for their tips, it was quite a job keeping them out of passengers' cabins long enough to get any work out of them.

As a distraction from my temporary disillusion with journalism, the *Southern Cross* couldn't have served me better. It had everything—larceny, petty and grand, rum-running, simple smuggling, complicated sex, and considerable physical violence. Only a few trips before I signed on, the then chief steward had been caught smuggling Chinese, and I was on hand myself the day the German stewardess got in a fist fight with my barber's manicurist, broke the vial of cocaine she'd been relying on, and so threw her into d.t.'s—or whatever the symptoms of sudden deprivation of a dope addict's stimulant are called. The poor manicurist went to pieces so fast that she was unable to get at her reserve supply, which was strapped to her body between her breasts and hips with a foot-wide band of adhesive tape. This hadn't been intended for her personal consumption anyway, being her stock in trade for the layover in New York.

It was really a very gay summer, and the most concentrated course in sophistication I have ever attended. Since every manifest on the boat was crooked—and I was anything but one of the gang—whenever we took on stewards' supplies, I was given a bottle of whisky and a sawbuck and told to take off and amuse myself. This was very kind of a management that made no particular effort to keep me from finding out what was going on. I had already been told that the last man to be indiscreet had been found wedged between the ship and a pier in Hoboken, allegedly the victim of an unhappy fall while the boat was docking.

And so, minding my own business, I got on very well with everybody, and after I got home I wrote a book about the trip. *The Saturday Evening Post* bought the first four chapters of it and published them under the title "Tips within Tips." My title had been "Thank You, Steward."

It was the practice on the *Southern Cross* to pool all tips given out in the stewards' departments to waiters, bedroom stewards, captains, deck stewards, and so on. The take was then reallocated, the chief steward helping himself to the biggest cut. The chef got the next, remainders dribbling down to include even scullery boys, whom no passenger had ever seen except when sunning themselves on the forecastle deck. This lore fascinated the editors of *The Saturday Evening Post*—thank goodness, because I didn't feel a bit like putting on paper some of the things I have set down here.

No one on the ship knew that I had pretensions to being a writer. But there are no secrets, and a couple of months after I left the *Southern Cross,* I got a telephone call from my old Chief Steward himself. He had been much too grand to associate with me on the boat. But now, here he was, asking if I would drop over to his hotel for a drink. Well, it was broad daylight and the hotel was in midtown Manhattan. I figured I could chance it, so I went around to see him. I had identified myself to the Munson Line's New York office—to get some facts I'd needed—and my secret was out.

"So you're going to write about us," the Chief Steward ruminated. "Well, that's quite a joke on us, isn't it?" I had my own notions of whom the joke would be on if he was seriously annoyed. He was a big florid man, very smooth spoken.

"I doubt if you'll be embarrassed," I told him hastily. "I'll be glad to show you the stuff."

"No," he said, "no, I'm not a curious fellow. I think you've got good judgment, son. But there is just one little incident I would kind of appreciate it if you'd overlook. I might even say it would be worth a year's supply of whisky to you."

This made me feel better and I remember wondering just what story it was he wished deleted. The last run we had made together had been a tense one. A careless pilot had taken a nick out of the starboard propeller, knocking it against the sea wall in Santos. After that we had had to limp all the way back to New York at half-speed. Since only about sixty per cent of the food and water that had been signed for had actually been taken on board—with the profit on the remainder split between the ship's chandler, the Skipper, and the Chief Steward himself—I had had to remake all the menus for the last week, serving every scrap of leftovers that could be reprocessed to make the larder last.

Or could the Chief be thinking about the knives that had been drawn during an argument between the Second and Third Stewards over the favors of a young college boy? But it turned out to be none of these things that bothered the Chief.

"I noticed," he said, "that you were on the town one night when we were in Rio—that night you ran into me at that Palace place. Oh, I could have been dancing, I suppose. You know how it is when you're away from home. But I don't think my wife would like to read about that kind of thing in a nice magazine. It wouldn't bother you much not to have seen me, would it?"

It didn't bother me a bit, and for months thereafter—every six weeks or so, in fact—I'd come home to find that someone had dropped off a case of Scotch at my door.

This is about the only adventure I ever remember telling Ross that I thought he envied a little.

As for me, I should most certainly have gone back for more, because I had enjoyed myself so much, but the encouragement from *The Saturday Evening Post* had gone to my head, and hell wouldn't have it but that I write a novel now.

If I had made my adventures on the *Southern Cross* into fiction, who knows? Instead, having dashed off what proved to be a *Post* article, I dedicated myself to higher things: specifically the writing of a psychological novel about a conflict between two women, a conflict involving the bearing of a child by one of them for the other's convenience. God knows where I ever acquired such a weird notion—or the mistaken confidence that I could give reality to a wholly imagined fable. But I was suddenly so convinced that I had something to say on the subject that I cashed in half my inheritance and rented a one-room penthouse apartment on East Fiftieth Street to write in.

Obviously only a penthouse would be appropriate, and I found one that could be had in those halcyon days for only seventy-five dollars a month. Through the fall and winter I labored over my typewriter to produce an opus called "Fair Exchange." Somehow the manuscript found its way—to the house of Knopf, I think it was—where a sister of the late Woodrow Wilson was a gentle and cultured manuscript reader.

She couldn't have been nicer about the whole thing. One of my minor characters, she felt, had come briefly to life for a few paragraphs . . . toward the end of the book. She told me that I should be encouraged by this. "But I *do* think it would be better," she added gently, "if we don't let anyone else see *this particular* manuscript."

I am sure I never told Ross about *this* incident. It would have given him too much pleasure. It was to become his strong conviction that the chances of my becoming a good editor depended upon my giving up my early ambition to write.

In point of time, I am now already past my first meeting with Ross at Katie Spaeth's, past also the appearance of Vol. I, No. 1 of *The New Yorker* itself. During the last weeks before it came out, I had been again approached with a plea to "go see Ross." This one had come from Nannine Joseph, the literary agent who had sold "Thank You, Steward" to the *Post*. Half prepared and now frantic, Ross had begun broadcasting all over town for help.

My decision was to wait and see whether I liked the first issue when it appeared. When it did come out, I was as dismayed as Knopf's reader had been by my novel. The names of most of the Algonquin group were there but none of their wit and sparkle. As a publication it seemed to me without form or discernible purpose.

In my arrogance, I gave Ross's magazine a few months' life at most, and got rid of the last two thousand dollars of my once precious hoard by buying a ticket on a boat sailing for Bordeaux.

I had vaguely in mind to spend the rest of my life in France. Thinking of becoming an expatriate was a phase through which every would-be writer in the twenties passed—whether to go on to glory or to retreat to a job as a broker's clerk. It was most definitely the thing to do.

But an even more important motive to me now was to find myself a wife.

XVI · The Makings of a Magazine

I went to Europe soon after Ross got *The New Yorker* started. I'll get back to what happened to me there—it's really part of another story. By my return, any kind of a job looked good to me; I was that broke by the early summer of 1925.

How the job I finally got turned out to be on *The New Yorker* made an anecdote that both Ross and I used to tell in variously embroidered versions, but the tag line, "Hell, I hire anybody!" was to become his slogan—and a basic ingredient of his formula for success.

It was altogether a confusing interview. Ross had agreed to discuss a job for me as a reporter; but now he said he didn't really know—maybe a reporter was the last thing he wanted. Clearly he was against trying me in particular in any role.

"I'll tell you . . ." Ross suddenly began again, throwing his arms wide in a sweeping gesture. But he never did tell me, because the gesture included an open bottle of ink, which he sent flying, the blue-black stuff cascading down the front of a new Palm Beach suit I had bought for the occasion.

That was the end of Round One, and I was ahead on points.

In Round Two, I scored a knockdown. Ross had rallied to explain that there simply wasn't such a person as the kind of reporter he had in mind. He would have to be a Richard Harding Davis and a Ward McAllister rolled into one.

"Well," I was able to interject, "I've been a reporter and Ward was my mother's uncle."

"Jee-sus," Ross snarled, as if completely disgusted with himself for having given me this opening.

Then a sigh escaped him, and he looked me sadly in the eye. "Okay, you're on," he said. "Hell, I hire *anybody!*"

The trouble with the way Ross had begun his magazine was that he hadn't "hired anybody." He'd gone in business still awed by the names that awed the members of the Thanatopsis Literary and Inside Straight Club, listing them proudly on page one as Advisory Editors: Ralph Barton, Marc Connelly, Rea Irvin, George S. Kaufman, Alice Duer Miller, Dorothy Parker, and Alexander Woollcott.

Of the seven, only the least known, Rea Irvin, was to play a working part in the creation of the magazine. In all fairness, Irvin's contribution might be said to have made up for all the others', for he is the man who made *The New Yorker*'s art what it is. But the rest of them were prima donnas.

What Ross needed most, faced with blank pages to be filled every week, was working editors with a creative understanding of what he was trying to do. The six "others" of his original board were a distinguished cartoonist, two playwrights, a novelist, a paragrapher, and a show-off. To most of them—and their friends—Ross was an amusing young man with a magazine into which they could empty their bottom drawers, exchanging manuscripts rejected by somebody else for Fleischmann's money —and thinking they were doing Ross a favor at that.

To help him handle these celebrities it must have amused the former editor of the *Stars and Stripes* to hire the son of "Blackjack" Pershing's Chief of Staff—Joseph Moncure March— as his first executive. Tall, dark, shy, and sensitive, Joseph Moncure had been a poet and was hopelessly miscast as a managing editor.

With the exception of March, almost everyone Ross relied on was better known than Ross himself; their attitude, always patronizing, was soon savagely critical. Fifteen thousand copies of the first issue had been sold under cover of a barrage of newsstand placards. Within the month, the circulation dropped to a frightening ten thousand. By the end of the second full month—that would be April—it was down to eight thousand, and the venture was costing more than that many dollars a week. By early May it was formally decided to cease publication.

The day was a Friday and another dreary issue was just going to press when Fleischmann called an emergency meeting at 11:00 A.M. at the Princeton Club. Only three men were invited: an Irishman named John Hanrahan, whom Fleischmann had engaged as "publisher's counsel" (Ross hated him), Hawley Truax, an original director of the F-R (F for Fleischmann, R for Ross) Publishing Company, and Ross himself. All three had been warned: the time when facts have to be faced has arrived.

The paper's original capitalization was long since gone. Each week's payroll and printing bill now came direct from Raoul's pocket.

Nor was there a single happy statistic in the house. Only half a dozen pages of advertising had been sold that week—including driblets classified under the heading "Where to Shop."

The magnificent build-up on this page ran, *"It is said confidentially by some of the smartest New Yorkers, that many of the shops listed on this page are the ones chiefly responsible for that very smartness! And you will well believe it, too, once you have investigated the cleverness and courtesy of these little* maisons—*for they are specialists in the felicities of the New York manner."* But the prominent little *maisons* included several establishments for the removal of superfluous hair, a corset hospital, and a place where a "Fiyu bob" (whatever that was) could be obtained for seventy-five cents.

Neither readers nor advertisers seemed anxious to share the financial burden of creating a new kind of wit. And what was there left that poor Ross could say? By noon, Fleischmann had reached his decision: there would be no more *New Yorkers*.

This decision—and how it came to be ignored—was already a legend when I arrived on the scene. The version I was brought up on had it that the meeting was a luncheon at which so many toasts were drunk that no one remembered to countermand orders for the printing of the next issue. The truth is more romantic than the fiction.

What actually happened was that Fleischmann, stalking grimly back to *The New Yorker*'s office after the meeting, overheard Hanrahan and Truax discussing what had just happened. Unable to keep up with his impatient stride, they had dropped a few paces to the rear, but somewhere between Fortieth and Forty-first Streets on Madison Avenue, Hanrahan's high voice carried clear: "God knows I don't blame Raoul, but it's like killing something that's alive, isn't it?"

It was the phrase "killing something that's alive" that stuck with the kindhearted Fleischmann. He couldn't quite forget it, and it was still on his mind when he showed up at Franklin P. Adams's wedding the next day. Adams, you will remember, was another charter member of the Thanatopsis Club, and all the old gang was on hand—including Ross himself. Unable any longer to bear his own thoughts, Fleischmann crossed the room to where Ross stood alone—and *The New Yorker* was alive again, for "one more try."

The program that was devised for this last-chance effort was an ingenious one. Acknowledging that the formula had not jelled, Ross was to be given the rest of the spring and all summer to set it straight. But during this period, instead of trying to improve the magazine each week, the whole editorial effort would be for the future—to gather material that could be concentrated in a new and improved *New Yorker,* which would begin with the first issue after Labor Day, the week that marked the opening of a new season in New York. In the interim, the less said about the magazine the better. It would be published for practice, as it were, without benefit of promotion or circulation effort.

Then for the fall issues, which would have the accumulation of four months' cream, the ringing sum of sixty thousand dollars was set aside to buy full-page advertisements in the New York papers. It was to be a concentrated *putsch* on all fronts, with September 12 the D-day. If *then* the public *still* did not respond —fair warning that *The New Yorker* would never see the new year.

Almost as important as Fleischmann's decision were the changes that had been taking place in Ross himself. The great disillusionment with his fancy friends had begun. For the first time Ross saw them for what they were, skillful and talented specialists in their own creative lines, but ineffective as creative journalists and cruelly quick to disassociate themselves from a venture whose failure might reflect on them. From this disillusionment Ross never completely recovered—and an important element of the ivory-tower journalism he taught his staff dates from it.

After April, Ross *did* hire anybody—and never again was he to rely on Great Names. Even his wartime friend Alexander

Woollcott felt the sting of his mistrust; when at long last Woollcott did become a regular contributor, it was despite Ross, not because of him.

So Ross hired anybody, and the first anybody was me. The next anybody was an equally unlikely character, a female by Boston out of Bryn Mawr, where she had played field hockey and edited *Tipyn o'Bob*. Boston and *Tipyn o'Bob* were bad enough, but Katharine Sergeant Angell's being a female broke every rule in Ross's book. Married to a Lucy Stone Leaguer himself—the Lucy Stoners were an ancient sect who believed in retaining their maiden names—Ross was passionately anti-feminist in his working household. (Women as contributors were in a separate category; Ross did not have to see them every day.) This was partly because he considered women emotionally unreliable, but particularly and specifically because it embarrassed him to swear in front of them, and it was impossible for him to operate without profanity.

Moreover, Ross enjoyed being intellectually rough on his associates. His characteristic criticism was sardonic, sarcastic, hard, sharp, merciless. His rages were prolonged, intemperate, and recurrent; and he would often beat people dozens of times over a period of months for the same mistake, sometimes keeping an offending piece of copy tacked up on the wall over his desk to remind him to get angry whenever he saw the perpetrator. Women very definitely cramped this style.

From experience, Ross knew that even the toughest of them was apt eventually to burst into tears—and that his own reaction would be to rush from the room, usually to hide out in a speakeasy for the rest of the day. He would be unable to decide with whom he was angrier, the hapless maiden for her tears or himself for having caused them.

So, as I say, the last thing Ross would have done in a reasonable mood would have been to hire a female to read manuscripts for him. He never made the mistake again while I was there. But it was a happy chance that he made it once—for the literary quality of *The New Yorker* is as surely, and as exclusively, Katharine Sergeant's as the flavor of the art is Irvin's.

It is another of the curiously paradoxical facts about Ross that as the creator of a great journal of letters he was almost illiterate himself. There is one important qualification to this statement. He was illiterate in the sense that his education in the English language had stopped in high school and that he had read little except newspapers since, nor could he express himself in any but the simplest words in the simplest of sentences, often run together in rambling incoherence. But so far as his education *had* gone, he was the most intense purist I ever knew.

Ross was—and was able to describe himself as—a grammarian. "God damn it, all I know about English is what I learned in a little red grammar and, Jesus Christ, this ain't it!" It was in passionate loyalty to his little red grammar that Ross came to hate Henry Robinson Luce and all his works. *Time*'s inverted sentences and cryptic captions had the same effect on him as a dentist's drill. So did Winchellisms. Perhaps what Ross sensed in Katharine Sergeant was a purist as pure as he; but Katharine was also an educated one.

I call Katharine "Sergeant" because it is the most Bostonian of her three names. When she came to work on *The New Yorker* she was married to a man named Angell, a nice quiet fellow whom she eventually divorced—for the sake of *The New Yorker,* I always thought, because her identification with the magazine was soon to become as complete as mine. Later on, Katharine was to marry *The New Yorker* literally as well as figuratively, in the person of E. B. ("Andy") White.

When this extraordinary woman first appeared in Ross's world, she brought more from Boston than its culture. She brought also a good solid chunk of its New England character. Ross was soon to find that while she was rather easier than most females to reduce to tears, their erosive effect on the granite of her decision was negligible. And when Ross ran away only to return in a penitent mood, she was quite capable of charging him for his tantrum. The cleaned-up barrack and barroom corn which Ross had once appreciated soon began to be conspicuous by its absence from the magazine.

Hard on Katharine's heels, in the succession of unlikely ones Ross was to hire, was the man she eventually married, the even mousier, milder, and gentler Elwyn Brooks White. Of all places, *he* came from an advertising agency. If there was anyone Ross hated working with more than a female, it was someone who had anything to do with advertising.

Curiously enough, Ross's own thinking on the subject of advertising was perceptive to the point of brilliance. *The New Yorker* owes its commercial success to this understanding. For the New York merchant-to-the-carriage-trade, Ross solved a problem up to then considered insoluble. This was how to avoid the waste circulation inherent in the mass readership of a metropolitan newspaper. Ross had it on paper before there was any *New Yorker* that *if* he could create a journal that could separate affluent sheep from penniless goats, stores with expensive merchandise to dispose of would love him forever.

But despite this extraordinary perspicacity, Ross regarded advertising, and anyone who had anything to do with advertising, with an unqualified loathing. In his own shop, he never ceased to resent the fact that an advertising salesman (who might be considered a moron) had to be paid several times the salary of a really gifted writer. The unctuous insincerity of advertising copy nauseated him, seemed an improper use of the English language, and his total dependence on the sale of advertising he regarded as a cross he was carrying to his own spiritual crucifixion.

So you can see how hard it must have been for him to give in and hire a young advertising copy writer. But, hell, I hire anybody!

Actually, Ross need not have feared, for E. B. White was spiritually even less of the advertising world than Ross himself.

More than anything else he was a poet, and, like Ross, had been a drifter. When the publisher of White's first book of poems asked him for a biography, he began his contribution:

"The poems of E. B. W. were written in places where Mr. White had gone in search of employment. When he graduated from Cornell in 1921 he found a job with the United Press. They sent him to cover the funeral of a statesman, but he took the wrong railroad, missing the cemetery by a scant forty miles. This terminated his connection with the U.P. and almost turned him against statesmen."

White's reference to his career with an advertising agency was equally pithy:

"He wrote a mail-order course in automobile salesmanship in ten easy lessons, but when the first order arrived from a barber in Wisconsin, he resigned, full of remorse. . . ."

Omitted entirely was the fact that he had grown up in Mount Vernon, New York, one of six children of a couple as gentle and charming as himself. His father was an executive in a piano-manufacturing company. Characteristically, White also left out of his biography his record as an editor of the *Cornell Daily Sun*. There he had won the Associated Press prize for the best undergraduate editorial of the year (it was on the use of correct English) and had been the subject of a eulogy by Arthur Brisbane. And it was because the first president of Cornell was named Andrew White that Elwyn Brooks there was, of course, called Andy.

But the really misleading note in White's blurb was the inference that as an advertising copy writer he had been unsuccessful. Actually, he did all right. There is practically no purpose to which words can be put that White would be unable to master —in writing. In speech he is hesitant, and his normal voice is almost inaudible. This inconsistency used to disturb him to a point where, in a recurring nightmare, he would dream that he was expressing himself as clearly in speech as in writing, turning out beautifully rounded and well-balanced sentences exclusively composed of words that were apt and discerning.

The New Yorker's editorial paragraphs (called "Notes and Comment") had originally been written by another brilliant young amateur named Filmore Hyde. But after Hyde drifted on, Andy took them over and gave them lasting fame. In effect, then, his correct title should have been Editorial Writer. The editor of *The New Yorker* himself never wrote an editorial for his own magazine that I know of. Once White took on the function of speaking for the whole, Ross would have been too much embarrassed to try to compete.

A generation ago, *The New Yorker*'s other great name, James (then James Grover) Thurber, was always linked with White's. This was because the public knew them first for the books they wrote together.

Thurber's original credentials were better than White's and infinitely superior to Katharine's or mine. He had come out of Columbus, Ohio, but had lived it down by working abroad— for the Nice edition of the Paris edition of the Chicago *Tribune*. He had also served as a code clerk in the American Embassy in Paris during the war and again at the Peace Conference. And most recently he had been a reporter on the New York *Evening Post,* where his specialty had been a kind of light color story not unlike *The New Yorker*'s own copy.

But despite this, Ross was anything but sure of his judgment in hiring him. Thurber was a weirdly unorthodox young man, tall and gangling, with a cascading mop of hair which kept falling forward and almost obliterating his face. He had lost the sight of one eye in a childhood accident and required thick glasses to focus the other; and he could outshamble and out-gesticulate even Ross himself. Moreover, he was a talker, which is always difficult for another talker to have around.

And as a talker Thurber was anything but ordinary, having a magnificent fluency and an ability to jog through hours of monologue, darting in and out of a score of subjects, and ending in double talk so cleverly contrived that it might be minutes after you had lost the gist before you realized that there was no longer any gist to follow. And he was a mad mimic, to boot, especially fond of confusing deceptions on the telephone. As a practical joker himself, Ross was for the first time well hoist with his own petard.

Set all this against the fact that Thurber's style and humor had a warmth and flavor that had never been in *The New Yorker* before and you have a fragment of the measure of Ross's confusion. It was a long time before he could decide whether hiring Thurber was his most brilliant achievement or his stupidest mistake.

Possibly the all-time low in Ross's judgment was when he came to an abortive conclusion that Thurber was no writer at all but should be made into an executive editor—a Jesus, no less! It took all of Thurber's wit to extricate himself from this misfortune—and I expect it was not long after the experience of trying to make an executive of Thurber that Ross made the first of several trips to Riggs Sanatorium in an attempt to recapture his sanity.

Thurber is also responsible for another black mark on Ross's record. Unamused himself, Ross for months refused to print a Thurber drawing—and never did give in until they first appeared as illustrations in Thurber's and White's book *Is Sex Necessary?*

Thurber's now-famous men, women, and animals first appeared as doodles on scratch pads, usually on someone else's desk. Thurber would stop by to see you when you weren't there, and on your return you would find whole pads full of his creatures leering at you. If you had a tablet to take down telephone conversations, for example, you would rip off the Thurber dog on the top page, only to find a Thurber seal on the next, and a man chasing a woman on the third—and so right on down to the cardboard back. It was very irritating.

Only White, who was Thurber's office roommate and must have suffered most, was amused. It was he who began to put captions to the more legible Thurbers and to submit them to the Art Meeting. But there Ross's veto was so violent that at first it shook everyone's judgment but White's.

Thurber was so deflated that he forbade his roommate to persist, and even rejected White's proposal that they try them on their book publisher. At this the indomitable Andy began his own collection of Thurber originals—by retrieving them from wastebaskets all over the shop, smoothing out the wrinkled copies, and pasting them on cardboard. These he took to the editors of *Harper's,* who were delighted with them. And so were the metropolitan critics when *Is Sex Necessary?* finally appeared. Reluctantly, Ross finally agreed to try a Thurber in *The New Yorker.* It was a sketch of a husband being berated by his wife in an old-fashioned bed, over the headboard of which a Thurber seal is observed balancing himself. The caption: "All right, have it your way. You heard a seal bark."

But again I have outrun my narrative. It was 1932 before all this came to pass. Neither Thurber nor White was there during the Summer of Trial. White wandered in in 1926; Thurber was hired in 1927. But Lois Long was there; I was present at the secret session in the summer of 1925 when she was hired away from Condé Nast's fancy-pants *Vanity Fair.* I think she had been the discovery of Joseph Moncure March. The departments that made her famous, and did a wheel-horse job of pulling *The New Yorker* through its first years, were "Tables for Two" and "On and Off the Avenue."

Then, as now, the first of these undertook to seek out the town's dining and wining places, the second to cover the fashion merchandise for sale in local stores.

What was pure Ross about *The New Yorker*'s concept of how to cover these fields was that both columns were to be dedicated to the buyer's interest rather than the seller's. They were, in effect, to be *anti*-advertising. This was important to Ross's soul, a small compensation to him for having to be supported by advertisers. So the formula called for a high acid content to cut the cloying claims that merchants and proprietors paid to print on other pages of the magazine. To insure her independence, the writer was to pay her own way, could accept neither free meals on the house nor gifts of merchandise.

If it is the rule that in making a magazine you can never hire the right person for the right job first time round, the young lady whom Ross engaged to translate this dream into reality was the exception that proved it. For Lois Long was almost unbelievably right from the first line she ever wrote; and thirty years later she is still unduplicatable.

Born a minister's daughter and briefly trained as a writer on *Vanity Fair,* in 1925 Lois was all zest and eagerness for the adventure of the big city. It was a happy coincidence for *The New Yorker*'s budget that Lois was an exceptionally good-looking girl as well as a gay and witty one, never at a loss for swains anxious to snub a management by paying her check. She had an almost infinite capacity for being childishly delighted with pretty things in stores, and with gay surroundings; her bubbly and insatiable appreciation never seemed to wear off.

But alongside this infectious quality of enthusiasm, at once underlying and flavoring it, Lois had a kind of native shrewdness, an ability to keep her head. She never quite lost touch with the reality that her world of glamour was for sale.

Thus in Lois were combined two rare ingredients: an ability to be perpetually stimulated, blended with an ability to be perpetually critical. It took just such a person to make Ross's rather stern and puritanical concept of journalistic honesty into weekly columns of words so readable and entertaining that they gave *The New Yorker* its first continuity of reader interest. The back-of-the-book service features, of which Lois Long's were the style-setting first, were exactly the keel that a magazine top-heavy with flashy wit needed to keep it on course.

The critical content of Lois's columns was also—set against the times—a daring journalistic innovation. This was particularly true in the merchandise-for-sale field. Few advertisers (or readers) at first believed it was on the up-and-up, and as Lois went right on speaking her mind hardly a week went by without the cancellation of some advertising as a result. Fleischmann and his advertising people were frantic, but Ross stuck by his guns. He said they would come back, and they did. They had to, for Lois's audience was to become so loyal that a line in her column could sell out a counter in a big department store, or make or break a new night club.

The same spirit of honest service also paid off in Ross's "Goings On about Town" column of the week's events, the blurbs for which had been written by the critics themselves since the first issue. There was no other place in town where you could find such a frank and convenient guide. The measure of Ross's success along these lines is testified to by the fact that a whole publishing venture—the magazine *Cue*—was presently to be founded on an expansion of this single function.

Ross's crusade for honesty in print even made some legal history, of interest at least to journalists. For instance, honest theatrical criticism is per se libellous. Clearly it damages the earning power of actors and producers—and a hundred years ago this was so held by the courts. Eventually this legal position was broken down by that process known as nullification—in the fields of theater and music, and in criticism of art. But in 1925 it was still intact in other fields, as *The New Yorker* discovered when it first printed a weekly critique of architecture.

New York was in the middle of a building boom, as frantic as the present scramble. To hold a new building's design up to ridicule was to damage its owner, its tenants, and its architect. *The New Yorker* found this out when its critic remarked that he had just inspected the new Fred F. French Building at Forty-fifth Street and Fifth Avenue and described the design as so unsound as to nauseate him.

We were immediately threatened with a suit—for millions; and again *The New Yorker*'s business people were in tears. Even

Ross, I think, was frightened then. But our brave writer, who was an architect himself, got affidavits from half a dozen famous friends—each affidavit to the effect that at a certain hour on a certain day each had found himself in the vicinity of the Fred F. French Building and experienced sensations of nausea which could be traced to no other cause. Several volunteered that they were unable to proceed until they had vomited. Confronted with the prospect of giving publicity to such evidence, the villains dropped the suit.

Another journalistic innovation—this one was first written by novelist Marcia Clark—gave critiques of new apartments being offered for rent. The worst trouble I remember with that one was when Marcia remarked that some new duplexes on Park Avenue were "so swell that even the maids use Chanel No. 5." That cost us the Chanel account for a few months.

But again I have run off my canvas. I should never have started talking about word people like Thurber and the Whites—or even Lois Long. The real beginnings of *The New Yorker* were not in its text, but in its pictures.

I have dropped the hint that a fellow named Rea Irvin is the man solely responsible for the distinctive quality of *The New Yorker*'s drawings. This is high praise, for *The New Yorker* most certainly revolutionized this century's humorous art. Yet the odds are that not one out of a thousand *New Yorker* readers has ever seen Irvin's name except in tiny hieroglyphics printed vertically in a corner of an occasional cover.

I can't vouch for the present, but for years and years every single picture *The New Yorker* printed was bought under Rea Irvin's watchful eye—and that despite the fact that he never had an office there nor was officially a member of the staff.

This extraordinary feat was accomplished at Irvin's own invention—a weekly gathering called the Art Meeting (it used to be held Tuesday afternoons) at which all art submitted during the last seven days was considered, rejected, sent back for revision, or bought. The board used to be Rea Irvin, Ross, Katharine White, and myself, and we sat on one side of a long table while Ross's secretary, Elsie Dick, sat on the other side and propped up pictures, one after another, for our comment, taking notes on what should be said to the artist.

By concentrating his work in a single afternoon, Rea Irvin was able to continue his altogether normal, easygoing life—and thus avoid the characteristic *New Yorker* neuroses. Irvin was older than Ross, with a distinguished career behind him before they met. A one-time cartoonist—at eighteen—for the San Francisco *Examiner,* Rea had been briefly an actor, then the inventor of his own comic strip. He was an art editor of the old *Life* when Ross found him.

As its one-afternoon-a-week art director, Irvin launched *The New Yorker* with the best work of illustrators already famous—to whom he opened up the magazine as a place where they could publish satirical pictures that no one else would print.

But Irvin's true uniqueness lay, and still lies, in the catholicity of his taste. Art editors, like artists, come bitter or benign, modern or classical, but are all traditionally unresponsive to the work of any school but their own. In dramatic contrast, Irvin's response was to see merit where merit lay, regardless of its artistic idiom. And the variety of styles and moods that he bought for *The New Yorker* gave its art a life and vigor that no other publication has yet matched.

In my time no member of the board ever talked to an artist until and unless he was one of the top half-dozen. This isolation of editors from aspiring artists was another facet of Ross's cowardice. He was terrified of having to argue with the poor fellows, to turn down their pictures, and so on. The minor executive to whom this unhappy assignment fell—and who held the job for years—was a sad young man by the name of Philip Wylie. He came to hate Ross for what he considered the latter's cavalier penny-pinching treatment of talent, and the experience may well

have laid the foundation for such bitter frustrated works as his
Generation of Vipers.

It was in August of 1925 that *The New Yorker's* circulation
dropped to its all-time low of 2,719. The weeks before the September 12 *putsch* were ticking away all too rapidly. We were
anything but ready when it came, and the first few heavily adver-
tised issues thereafter hardly took the town by storm.

In the end, I have always felt that it took luck to put *The New
Yorker* across. Not luck in general, but one specific piece of luck
—in the form of an unsolicited article which put us on the front
page of every newspaper in New York and made us, for a few all-
important weeks in November and December, literally the talk of
the town.

The article was a journalistic freak. One of the best-known
names in New York at the time was that of Clarence Mackay, a
second-generation tycoon and now chairman of the board of
Postal Telegraph. He had a daughter named Ellin whom he had
recently introduced to New York society in considerable style.
Since she was a pretty girl, too, the society editors had made her
into a celebrity. But Ellin had a mind of her own. She was against
the whole business and sat herself down to say so in fifteen hundred rebellious words, which she entitled "Why We Go to Cabarets—A Post-Debutante Explains." For some obscure reason,
Ellin then had this document bound in leather and sent around to
the brash young *New Yorker* to publish.

I have a vivid memory of finding this exhibit on my desk one
morning—with a scribbled note from Ross reading, "What
think?" To keep my judgment pure, he had removed the title
page with Miss Mackay's name on it.

In my embryonic career as a *New Yorker* editor, it was a historic moment when I wrote back "It's a *must.*" The girlish prim-
ness of the piece was hardly in *The New Yorker* idiom, but as a
document it was genuine—and genuinely provocative. The
theme: that nice young girls were being driven to cabarets be-

cause they resented being put on the auction block at debutante parties; and besides, the stags they met there were bores. Hardly breath-taking, but it was marvelous medicine for a magazine that had been advertising itself as a sophisticated social critic.

I knew the piece would cause all kinds of talk, whoever wrote it. It did; even the New York *Times* picked it up. We kept the pot simmering for weeks with a "Retort Courteous" that I got a friend of mine in the Racquet and Tennis Club to write, and then a final rejoinder from Miss Mackay.

The following year, Miss Mackay demonstrated her further good sense by marrying Irving Berlin, the young song-writer— giving one more round of publicity to the magazine in which she had declared her independence from Park Avenue.

By the time we were through with the Mackay hoopla, for all practical purposes the magazine was over, its circulation bouncing from less than three thousand to almost thirty. Its December 12 issue was a bulging fifty-six pages. There had been only twenty-four in the issue before the *putsch;* most of the difference was in paid advertising.

All of this is much too smugly put, in the happy security of hindsight. By the end of its first year of publication everyone concerned with *The New Yorker* had been too abused by ridicule— the early *New Yorker* had been every wit's target—to feel the slightest breath of security. Moreover, the magazine was still losing buckets of Fleischmann's money on every issue. Its advertising rates had been based on only twelve thousand circulation, and these bargain rates of a hundred and fifty dollars a page had been guaranteed to advertisers for another year. Ross still felt the devil at his heels, and drove us all with a frenzy I doubt if any of us has ever forgotten.

The heart of Ross's own anxiety was his seriously taken opinion that in the whole United States there was not produced, in a single week, enough first-class material to fill a small magazine. Hence he was committed to publishing not what he really wanted to publish, but simply what he disliked least.

I can't remember a piece by anyone but E. B. White that Ross ever really thought just right. White was the exception to prove his lack of faith in everyone else. White was his darling and could do no wrong. But Andy was as stubborn about being no man's man as Ross was. He once refused an attempt by Ross to triple his salary, and later resigned and went over to write for *Harper's*. It was not that Andy didn't love Ross; it was just that he didn't want to belong to him, and Ross was very hurt and felt that he was being abused.

Possibly Ross got over this, but in the years I knew him, in his personal relations outside the office Ross was often unbelievably naïve. He once got so excited about the possibilities of a new kind of paint sprayer that he put all the money he had in it —and lost it, of course. And there was the much-publicized incident of the male secretary he hired "to keep those God-damned women out of my office"—who succeeded in stealing ten or twenty thousands of his money and losing it on the horses before Ross caught up with him.

As to Ross's emotional life in his early days, from a girl I once knew I have this firsthand story of Ross's attempt to seduce her. It was in the early twenties, and when she accepted his dinner invitation she found Ross had taken a private room in a speak-easy and decorated it with flowers on the table and champagne in a bucket. She was a very sophisticated girl, and this vastly amused her. At the end of dinner, Ross circled the table for the obvious purpose of embracing her. They did several times around the track before she dropped into a chair, hysterical with laughter.

At this Ross is described as breaking into tears, asking if she could ever forgive him—and running out the door.

I believe this story implicitly. Ross was the most moral of men, to the point of prudishness. Month after month it was preached to us, "This is a family magazine, for Christ's sake!" The only double meanings that got into the book were ones that Ross didn't understand.

Normally shy about interviewing prospects until they'd been screened, Ross once indulged himself by taking on a young Vassar graduate who had sent her name in, asking to see the editor about a job. Toward the end of her sales talk, the poor girl had the misfortune to comment that of course she "understood what might be expected of a girl—after all, I guess, a magazine about Broadway isn't very different from Broadway itself. . . ." Ross again fled the room, called a formal staff conference, and bawled hell out of all of us for half an hour, for the kind of impression we were making on the public.

I was once so close to Ross, and he was such an extraordinary man, that you will now understand my obvious reluctance at trying to sum him up. Ross is a uniquely difficult subject to get on paper. To write about him at all is to feel him leering over one's shoulder, as he is leering over mine right this minute.

XVII · Dream's End

It was my bankrupting myself in Europe, you may remember, that brought me to Harold Ross's door in the first place, hat in hand, seeking a job. And it was the pursuit of a maiden from one end of Europe to the other that had done the bankrupting. I must tell that story before I forget.

The time it happened was the winter and spring of 1925, just after *The New Yorker*'s first appearance.

The object of my affection at that time was a girl I had known since childhood. Her name was Eleanor and we had climbed arbors together when we were two. Then I hadn't seen her again until we were in our early teens, at which time I decided that everything about her was repulsive. She was almost as tall as I, even awkwarder—and I think wore braces on her teeth. Also, her mother having been an Emmet, she had the status of a semi-cousin, that is, someone I was supposed to be nice to. I said she was spinach, and meant it.

But time passes, and when we were both seventeen we found ourselves together again, and I kissed her (the braces were gone) —out of custom. Some minutes later she fled, laughing over her shoulder, "See what you've missed all these years!"

What I had missed, I soon found, was not the necking, but a gay and witty companion; also an available one, because unlike Constance Clarke, Eleanor was never the belle of a ball. She hadn't the looks or the figure, and didn't get to many balls either, because her branch of the Emmet family lacked the Christopher Temples' trust funds.

Eleanor and her widowed mother lived alone in a flat on lower Fifth Avenue, down near Twelfth Street, and she made her own dresses. So she went on my list as the girl I took out because we had fun together, and because, when I was lonely, I knew she was always there.

It was the time I was first faced with the fact that she might not always be there that I began thinking about Eleanor seriously.

That was the fall I tried writing my novel. I went up to Salisbury to see my family and, of all people, found Eleanor there. She was stopping for lunch with an old friend of my father's, a fabulous female character from Chicago whose nickname was "Ri-ti-ti," or, translated from the Chinese, Great Living Thunder. The plot of the piece was that Ri-ti had invited Eleanor to go around the world with her, as a kind of de luxe all-expenses-paid companion.

Ri-ti was very rich and maintained houses in Shanghai and in Paris and in a couple of places in the United States—Palm Beach

I think one of them must have been. Her husband had gone down on the *Titanic;* Ri-ti had been there, too, but everyone agreed that she had been unsinkable. And now she had "discovered" Eleanor, whom I had considered my personal possession, and was about to launch her on a career of glamour, beginning with a World Cruise! It must have given me quite a pang.

Anyway, what I did about all this was to note carefully the date on which the cruise was due to arrive at Monte Carlo in the Mediterranean. Ri-ti, of course, was planning all kinds of stop-overs, so they would not get there until the following February. Then I took Eleanor to one side and said something like, "Look! When my novel is done, why don't I go over and meet your boat?" And Eleanor said, "Well, why don't you?" So that was that, a casual kind of commitment to meet again, four months later, four thousand miles away. It appealed to the romantic in me.

But writing a novel, even a bad one, is a lonely business, and long before the four months were up I found myself missing Eleanor more than I imagined I could. A girl to sleep with might be managed at that age, but a girl who was fun to talk with was something else again. I was over Constance—but what next?

It was at this juncture that the whole puzzle seemed suddenly to fit together for me. The only girl I had ever really wanted had been Constance. But it hadn't worked out because I had been too much in love with her. Q.E.D., best marry the someone you are simply most fond of—someone gay, and with the same sense of humor as yours; someone with whom you have never been bored; someone you admire for her own sake, whose courage is clear, and whom you've never heard complain. Lord! . . . why hadn't you thought of it before! Eleanor's the perfect wife for you! Take ship at once and explain all this to her—and after that it will be the two of you against the world.

I think that's a pretty good reconstruction of how I reasoned it out. And when I had made my decision—it about coincided with Woodrow Wilson's sister's decision that my novel was not for this world—I felt very happy.

I had had no word whatever from Eleanor, but that didn't bother me. I simply cabled her that I'd be there in Monte Carlo waiting—what better proof of devotion could she have—and sold the last of my stocks to buy a ticket on a boat that would land me in Bordeaux a week before hers was due to dock an overnight train ride away.

I wonder what would have happened to my life if I'd written a short story about Eleanor instead of a novel about two women I've never met? I might have turned into a writer instead of whatever I am. Because I came to know Eleanor very well.

Anyway, ours was a funny love story—with an unhappy ending. Only the setting was solid stuff; it was the purest of pure twenties: two young Americans in Europe, living like millionaires on inflated francs, gambling their getaway money at Monte Carlo, flying the Mediterranean to Corsica, riding all night on the roof of a passenger train from Marseilles to Paris in the rain—just because it was fun—celebrating the sale of a story by spending the whole proceeds in an evening—things like that. The same kind of kids couldn't do it now, because the confidence is gone.

Take my own trip over, which is where the first tragicomic complications began. Two nights out, I learned the name and address of a farmer near Cassis (halfway down the Cote d'Azur from Marseilles) who had put up two young American artists, board and lodging, in a stone cottage looking over the harbor for a whole year for five hundred dollars. Bang! My decision was made to spend the next five years there—and in the end I almost did! It could only have happened then.

But that wasn't what made the complications. It was a case of pneumonia. I came down with it first halfway across the Atlantic. A French ship's doctor cured me of that spell by scrubbing my chest with steel bristles until it bled. At Bordeaux I was barely strong enough again to walk ashore and climb into a second-class compartment on the night train to Nice. Still under the illusion that the Riviera was a warm and sunny winter resort, I had brought only summer clothes. It was a frosty night, and the train unheated. By morning I was barely conscious, knew that I had a high fever, and was running in and out of delirium. Concentrating hard, I persuaded a taxi in Nice to drive me to the "best hotel." My penny-conserving plan had been to stay in pensions, but I knew I had better be somewhere I would be taken care of, or else.

That was how I came to miss Eleanor's boat entirely—for I was clean out of my head and being nursed by a kindly chambermaid the day it docked. It was the kindly chambermaid who pulled me through—with hot flatirons to warm my feet and hot tea to sustain me. I got better. Better enough to learn what day it was—oh my God, I've missed Eleanor!—and to send letters and telegrams hoping to catch up with her. Then after another day I was suddenly well again. Weak but quite well. At twenty-four it can be like that.

I got all dressed up. I bought flowers. I hired a huge limousine —to drive me to an address I had for Eleanor in Menton. Ri-ti had a brother living there, and her party was to have left the cruise boat in Monte Carlo to visit him.

When I arrived in Menton, I found Ri-ti's brother easily enough—in a pretty villa in the hills—but no Eleanor. The cruise party had broken up, and Eleanor had moved to a small hotel in town. And it was the day after that before I caught up with her.

It was a truly touching reunion. Eleanor was marching up and down the courtyard like a caged lioness. "So it's you . . . at last!" She had received none of my letters or cables and knew I was in Europe only because—of all things!—while riding in a bus she had looked up to see me passing in my limousine, dressed to kill and carrying flowers for she knew not whom. Or cared, she said.

She had a story of her own to tell.

Between this meeting and our last in Salisbury had lain four months of hell with Ri-ti. The glamorous invitation had proved to be a sham; she'd been expected to be Ri-ti's unpaid maid, and Ri-ti herself had disclosed an arrogance that, en route to the West Coast the first week, had caused a Pullman porter to quit the train and his job rather than continue to take her abuse.

Somewhere in the Orient, Eleanor had fallen ill, and the party had gone on without her, abandoned her in a cheap hotel room lit by a single hanging electric bulb. When she was well enough to travel again—weeks later—she had followed Ri-ti's ship into Monte Carlo solely for the purpose of speaking her mind to her onetime patroness. That, too, was like her, because Eleanor had both solid character and a fierce pride.

Now she was on her own, living on the last of the mad money her mother had given her, and grimly determined to salvage some pleasant experience out of the round-the-world debacle.

We had been drinking—porto, I think—on the hotel terrace while I had been learning these things. I felt sorry for what had happened to Eleanor, but basically very smug. It was all over now, wasn't it? And *I* was there, I, too, having overcome obstacles to keep the tryst. Surely it *was* a tryst; Eleanor hadn't come half-way round the world from Hong Kong solely to give Ri-ti her comeuppance.

I decided to let her in on the secret.

I said, and God forgive me, "Eleanor. You know I don't love you, but let's get married."

The trouble with Eleanor's giving me *my* comeuppance was that after she was through I was still there, and she was still there, and we were alone together in a foreign country. And the evidence is that she *had* been in love with me, and I probably with her, for all my fatheadedness. Nothing else could explain how either of us handled the situation.

For the next two months we lived together—in separate hotels. That is, we spent our days together, ate only with one another, made our plans and traveled together. Only, by the end of each

and every evening—and often that end hardly came before dawn
—we contrived as if by mutual agreement to get into an argument over nothing, and leave each other in a huff. And only the
next morning to meet, elevenish, over a porto, to pick us up, and
thereafter to spend as happy days as I can remember, on beaches
and in gay restaurants, walking, talking, doing whatever pleased
us.

No one but a careful student of the times would believe that
we never slept together, but we didn't. After her first refusal, I
was more determined than ever to stick it out. I would wear her
down with my devotion. But damned if I would ever lie to her—
truth seemed to me the essence of what we had together—by saying that I loved her. Because I knew I did not. What I felt bore
no resemblance to the gnawing need I had had for Constance—
thank God!

And so it went the whole of that spring—until we were both
really without funds, present or expected; and took ship together,
sailing back as from a dream to reality.

XVIII · And So to Matrimony

The story of Eleanor is proof that in my youth I was an idiot. It was in the clear dawn light of disillusion—with my inability to work out a satisfying life for myself or anybody else, and stony broke—that I finally hustled around to take Ross's job.

It was after my first total absorption with this job had passed that I got back, as it were, to thinking about my emotional life and what I was going to do with it. I felt very old because the calendar said I was almost twenty-five. But this time, instead of having twenty-four hours a day on my hands in which to mull over the mystery of my existence, any thought of myself had to be snatched at odd moments from the uncompromising demands of my masters, Mr. Ross and his magazine.

The early New Yorkers were late risers and drifted into West Forty-fifth Street around ten. But I was usually there—if Ross hadn't sidetracked me for breakfast—at 8:30, so as to get an hour or two of work done before the telephone began ringing. And lunch was my time for being out gathering material for the "Talk of the Town."

I had a technique and a routine for this which I recommend to young reporters. I was going to say that I invented it, but recall it now as the helpful suggestion of a young public-relations counselor named Edward L. ("Eddie") Bernays.

The problem was to keep track of a dozen different highly specialized fields of endeavor. Said Bernays, "In each world there's always one gossipy individual who makes it his or her business to know everything. Sometimes they're the biggest people in the business, but more likely they're frustrated second-stringers or some boss's secretary. You go find them and offer each this trade: the low-down in *his* field for what you know about what's going on elsewhere in town. Part of the trade is that you buy him lunch once a month. But don't rely on the lunch—or your charm—to get you what you want; you must pay off in sound money—in a world in which gossip is legal tender."

It took me a few months to set up my board of gossips, but after I had them I was in business. For the theater I had the play-reader for a leading producer; the daughter of a diva kept me posted on music. It was about then that I ran into a young former vaudeville hoofer named Walter Winchell whose column showed more evidence of hard work than anyone else's in town. We used to do our trading at lunch at the Yale Club—Walter got up in time for lunch those days. Since he gathered his information by night and I by day, in a way we covered both sides of the street;

and the kind of thing I used in *The New Yorker* was not competitive with his crisp condensations.

I have been party to a lot of arguments about Winchell since those days—and long after my time, *The New Yorker* itself was to print the savagest of attacks on him as an institution. But it remains my solid conviction that he is an honest journalist and that the real secret of his success was—and is—simply hard work. It has been thirty years now, and no columnist in the United States has successfully competed with him. I believe that this is because he has consistently been more curious, and worked harder to satisfy his own curiosity—and hence his public's.

I have heard Winchell called everything from a blackmailer to a paranoiac, but if he had been either, he could never have survived. Yet Ross—who had basically the same curiosity and drive, and the same dedication to the truth as he saw it—always hated Winchell. Primarily, as I have said, this seemed to be for the same reason he hated Luce, for lese majesty toward English grammar. But Ross also lived by the prudish principle that a journalist might—must—crash any door except the one that led to a bedroom. He had an almost pathological aversion to the kind of journalism that printed news of pregnancy or divorce.

The afternoon hours on *The New Yorker* were usually the busiest for me, but by somewhere around six or six thirty, most of the stenographers and secretaries had managed to escape—barely, because we would have liked everything in the shop retyped every day in Ross's mad pursuit for perfection. Thereafter it was the invariable custom for most of the staff to move on to whichever was the favorite speak-easy that year, to continue working the magazine over, this time with the helpful assistance of bootleg whisky.

The time *The New Yorker* staff—and its contributors—spent in speak-easies was something that concerned Ross so deeply that he eventually decided that we ought to have a speak-easy of our own. And then, as usual with such notions, it fell to my lot to provide it. It proved an educating experience.

Among the few assets Fleischmann had been able to keep out of *The New Yorker*'s pot were several parcels of real estate on West Forty-fifth Street. One was the office building at 25 where we worked; another was an office building just down the other side of the street. So Fleischmann was talked out of its basement, and some secondhand furniture was bought, including a fine old mahogany bar. Then we hired ourselves a combination bartender and bootlegger, and we were in business.

It was to be a kind of club without dues. Invitations were extended only to contributors we thought worth encouraging. You were supposed to be Somebody if you got one.

Running hazily through Ross's brain was the notion that he was creating an institution that would emulate *Punch*'s famous literary salons. He had incidental information from London that the way the editors of *Punch* perpetuated themselves as a group was by fraternizing with favored contributors, from whom, eventually, new editors would be chosen. *The New Yorker* speak-easy was thus to be a twentieth-century American version of a nineteenth-century English institution. As such it was an inglorious fiasco.

In the first place, the right contributors—the Benchleys and the Parkers—took one look at our self-conscious creation and went rapidly back to the even dingier haunts they loved so well. The artists we wanted so much to talk with never even took the one look; they were much too shy. That left only the more adventurous freeloaders. (People were supposed to be charged for their bottles by the bootlegger-bartender, but since he was underwritten by the management, not many collections were made.)

All this had been accurately predicted by other sophisticates as qualified as I—but Ross would believe none of us and stubbornly insisted on keeping open until the one thing that could make him change his mind happened: sex got into the act.

As the nominal proprietor, it was my custom to drop in on our speak-easy each morning on my way to the office, just to see that everything was in order, and our one employee on hand, as he was supposed to be, tidying up from the night before. On the last morning *The New Yorker* speak-easy ever opened, I showed up around nine and let myself in upon the opening scene of a play written and staged by Dali.

In the center of the stage were chairs neatly piled on tables. Up right, behind the bar, our dour and taciturn handyman was solemnly polishing glasses, stacking them in a pyramid before him.

And up left, pulled out from the wall for the obvious purpose of making it more convenient for the mopping of the floor, which had just been completed, one sofa—on which stretched two of our contributors, stark naked in each other's embrace, and out colder than two mackerels, one male, one female.

The stunned silence in which my mouth fell open at what I thought might be an apparition was broken by the bartender's rather sorrowful voice. Gesturing with a glass toward the sofa he asked me, "And where would you like me to put those, sir?"

To a definitely cheeseclothed version of this tableau, given him in his office some hours later, Ross reacted by turning the premises back to Fleischmann within the hour. As like Queen Victoria as two peas in a pod, he was not amused—and obviously it was *my* fault because, God damn it, I knew better than to let a thing like that happen.

Much gayer and sometimes even great fun were the annual beer parties that succeeded the speak-easy. It seems to me that the first we held was down in Webster Hall. Because it was such a big place, we could ask assorted celebrities and friends as well as our dreary selves and our contributors. Also the office help had a really fine time, getting looped among the great and the near-great. My favorite memory is of a tiny secretary approaching Mr. Gene Tunney, then heavyweight champion of the world, and announcing in a clear voice, "Sir, I introduce myself because it has always been my ambition to rub elbows with the great." Considering the champion's own formal manner of expression, this was very likely the young lady's idea of the insult supreme. But

Mr. Tunney won everyone's heart by turning solemnly and advancing his right elbow—to be rubbed.

My own relation with most of the galaxy of stars among whom we circulated was just as impersonal. Ross's book was my bible then, and it was his belief that the fine edge of critical wit could only be dulled by social contact with the people one wrote about. One might get to like some of them! That would be awful.

So, in a way, if you had time to think about it—which you hadn't—it was really a lonely kind of life. Which is, possibly, the reason why within the year I began to think again of getting married.

This time around I had nothing specific in mind—that is, I was without any formula at all, even a silly one. But life seemed to be streaming by and I standing still. Also, I recall feeling a very definite urge to have a life of my own with more in it than simply a room to come home to, a room that was no longer the fortress I'd built from which to go forth to conquer, but now simply a place where there was a bed on which I could rest for a few hours before going back to the only life I had, at my desk in *The New Yorker's* office.

It was not that I was as yet discontented with that life. In it, for the first time I felt really useful and needed and satisfyingly important. Rather, it was a growing awareness that in my furious functioning I was more machine than human being.

So, moved by some vague feeling of incompleteness, I showed up one evening at the kind of occasion I had not been part of since my New Haven days: a coming-out party for somebody I didn't know.

I went professionally, of course, telling myself that I wanted to see what it was still like back in that world. As I might have expected, it seemed a children's party to me—rather pleasant to watch, making me feel a little nostalgic, even—from the giddy altitude of my middle twenties. But it was certainly nothing I regretted having outgrown.

To pass the time, I cut in to dance with a very young girl who looked fresh and gay and graceful. She wasn't the prettiest on the floor, but she had an alert and eager look about her and clearly sensitive eyes and mouth. She had brown hair but very fair skin.

After we danced a while, I introduced myself and she said that her name was Elizabeth but that she called herself Tommy —for some reason she couldn't remember, because she didn't think she was the tomboy type. I found her so easy to talk with that we spent the rest of the evening together.

As I have said, Tommy was far from the season's prettiest girl, but there was something about her—I think it was her eagerness to begin living—that caused males around her to react very strongly. By the following spring I, too, found that I was reacting, above and beyond, etc.—and asked her to marry me.

She said she would—and six months later did.

Tommy's full name was Mary Elizabeth Carden. Her father was "Judge" George Alexander Carden, and he was a really extraordinary figure, truly worth his own biography. Born in Opelika, Alabama, he had graduated from law school while still in his teens, and had then migrated to Texas and made—and lost—his first million while still a boy. Thereafter he continued to make—and continued to lose—larger and larger sums until by 1925, when he was in his sixties, his most recent disaster had involved six or seven million and made headlines in the New York press.

Judge Carden was one of the last of a generation of financial buccaneers that went out with the bull markets of the twenties and the coming of the Securities Exchange Commission. But he was curiously atypical in that he was more liberal intellectual than man of property. He was a voracious and continuous reader on serious subjects and had deep convictions on social reform. The social-security laws of the New Deal he considered the greatest single step taken by mankind since the coming of Christianity, and near the end of his life he was to help draft the legislation which created that very S.E.C. that put him out of business.

But in finance the Judge was as ruthless, as daring, and as cavalier as a Mississippi River gambler was supposed to have been. He once told me that the secret of success in losing money was never to lose too little; if you go enough millions into the red, your creditors will have no choice but to stake you again; only chance they have to get their money back.

The businesses in which the Judge had operated—the Judge part was a courtesy title from his Texas years—included oil (of course), sulphur, real estate, radios, air conditioning, and sometimes bizarre side lines like Eskimo Pie. From a wartime sally into the shipping business he had acquired a tantalizing asset in the form of a twenty-five-million-dollar claim against the United States government for unpaid profits. The suits that were filed in connection with it were in court for years and were so legally fascinating that the late John W. Davis once offered to handle one on a contingent basis.

I can't remember how John W. came out, but some of the suits were won, and several million in cash collected. However, most of the money had long since been spent on lawyers' fees and the political payoffs required to get the necessary bills through Congress. (For an individual to sue the government, a special Act of Congress is required, authorizing the suit.)

But all this government-suit activity was a kind of side line— and a sustaining dream—to the Judge, whose principal operations when I knew him were on the security and commodity exchanges. Just before Tommy and I met each other, one of his stock pools had gone wrong and he had been forced to liquidate half a dozen seats on the stock exchange and a lot of other things. But he still had his duplex apartment on Park Avenue and a big old-fashioned house on Long Island near Bay Shore, and his formula of rehabilitating himself on his creditors' money was working all right again. He was on his way back via control of a nationally known electrical-supply house.

None of this was I to learn until sometime after Tommy and I were married. Partially this was because I was so preoccupied with *The New Yorker* and partially because at that time and age I considered the marriage of two young people none of either of their parents' business—really. I never gave the Judge and Aunt Rose much of my valuable time before annexing their daughter.

Aunt Rose was as extraordinary in her way as the Judge. She had been the sweetheart of her husband's youth, but he had married Another Girl. So she had waited, supporting herself as a court reporter, for ten or twenty years—until he had raised three daughters by his first wife and been left a widower and come back for her. She always knew he would. Then she bore him three more children, of whom Tommy was the second.

Aunt Rose was a pretty, gentle woman, tiny and very feminine. Married to a gambler, she hated gambling and the uncertainties of a gambler's life. But the Judge could do no wrong. The Judge himself was a small man, delicately made, and his distinguishing feature was his enormous dark eyes, intense, luminous, as beautiful as any woman's. They were set wide in a handsome, very masculine face—his skull could have been a model for Julius Caesar's—and seemed literally to burn with an inner fire. He was a beautiful talker and gracious and courtly in his manners. It was easy to see how the Judge had managed to be so effective; what was harder to understand was how a man of such extraordinary and effective intelligence had succeeded in ruining himself so many times. Mathematically, he was almost a genius; he certainly knew the odds he played.

I have to stop myself from writing on about the Judge and Aunt Rose, because eventually they came to fascinate me, and I was deeply fond of them. They are both long dead. And as I've said, I had no idea at the time that I was marrying into such an interesting family.

Tommy and I pledged our troth privately while walking the ties of a freight yard in New London. We were on our way back from watching a boat race—for *The New Yorker,* of course. It was June, and our idea was to get married right away. But first there was the convention of an announced engagement to be bowed to, and then came Ross's ulcerated tooth and my crack-up. For that was *that* summer. When I set its story in context with *The New Yorker*'s, I forgot to mention that I was engaged to be married at the time. So it wasn't exclusively overwork that laid me out; it was overwork plus a biologically unsound postponement of nuptials. I have had a scunner against long engagements ever since.

There is also a side light on my employer, Harold W. Ross, in the story of that summer. Since it was a foundation stone of Ross's journalism that a citizen's personal life was his own business, it hadn't even occurred to me that I should take Ross into my confidence about mine. So when he read of my engagement in the press, it was the first news he had had on the subject. His dumbfounding reaction was to blow his top! I had no right to take such a step without consulting him . . . I was crazy . . . I was going to ruin a life he thought might have promise. It was even worse than that. It was—God damn it, there wasn't any other way of putting it—just plain *disloyal!*

This tirade—these tirades, for they went on and on and on— had just about as much effect as a saner man could have expected, that is, none, or, rather, none on my decision to marry whomever I pleased, whenever I pleased; but they did do a great deal to our personal relationship, now that Ross was casting himself in the role of the father who knows best how his son should live his life. It did not take my subconscious long, I suspect, to confuse him with that other father who had seemed so omnipotent in my childhood, and to resent him just as bitterly. When I had my crack-up, some of my most consoling daydreams were of how to dispense with Ross once and for all—by garroting, disemboweling, or simple shooting in the head with a forty-five.

Looking back on those violent, emotional times, the thing that seems extraordinary to me is that I was able to survive them, with only a woodpile to help me work off my aggressions.

Anyway, that's the way it happened. Like her mother before

her, but for hardly so long, Tommy waited it out while I disappeared from her life to wrestle with my soul. She came up to the country to see me once, but all I could tell her was that I was in no fit shape now to marry anybody.

But when I had myself in hand again Tommy was still there, and we had a very fancy wedding in the chapel my mother and father had been married in. It was complete with appropriate costumes, including top hats and cutaway, and a monster of a reception at the Plaza Hotel.

All this struck Ross as so amusing that he almost broke up our receiving line when he went into gales of uncontrollable laughter on being formally announced to the principals by the Cardens' butler. And he got me laughing so, with his rubber gargoyle of a face and his madly vertical hair, that the whole bewildered wedding party became suddenly infected, and all Tommy's crinkly bridesmaids and my starched and tailored ushers began suddenly to snicker, too—so that the lot of us were presently roaring with laughter at we knew not what. It was as if the cast of a too-serious play were suddenly to see themselves through a mischievous gremlin's eyes and to break into hysterical laughter in the middle of their lines.

Then it was over, and we sobered back into our politely social roles. As far as I can remember, that was the first and last time Ross and Tommy ever met. But in holding himself aloof from my home life, Ross was making no real exception. He was a rare social guest of any of his executives those days. At least after the wedding, he was gracious enough to give me time off for a honeymoon—six whole days.

Having overcome such a formidable obstacle as my emotional involvement with *The New Yorker,* Tommy and I felt that we were entitled to a little peace and normality, at least for the few hours I could spend away from the office. And I think we would have done all right, as young couples go, for we were very happy together and a great comfort to each other—and our personal life together was as gratifying and as exciting as it should have been—but for the sudden onset of another physical catastrophe, this time Tommy's.

We were still bride and groom, a scant two months married, when my wife fell ill with an infection of unexplained origin which was to hospitalize her for most of our first year of marriage. It was an internal thing, threatening her with a hysterectomy. I fired seven doctors in succession to keep them from performing one, in the end betting on the opinion of a drunken Scotsman.

In the last crisis I could only catch up to this individual via ship-to-shore telephone, interrupting a very gay party on his yacht; he was a very rich and unorthodox gynecologist. He had been one of half a dozen consultants. Uninhibited now, he gave me his frank opinion of his famous associates who were so anxious to get busy with knives, and predicted that my wife would get well in a month if they would only leave her alone. And she did. But only a few months later she fell ill again.

This time my adversary was much more formidable. It was pulmonary tuberculosis, a disease to which Tommy must have inherited her susceptibility, for two of her older half-sisters had already contracted it, and one was to be invalided by it most of her life.

That was the end of the ball game, so far as Tommy and I ever leading the kind of life they write about in popular magazines. Together we fought something much more real than potential triangles and the servant problem. We fought death, living with us as an accepted member of the household.

After each hard-won recovery—there were no miracle drugs in those days—we would have a few months of cautious life. But always these happy interludes would end with another lesion.

XIX · Manhattan Nightmare

All these and a lot of other things happened to Tommy and me in the years when I was Ross's managing editor. But if there was a grimness about those years, they were rarely unhappy. The struggle for Tommy's life brought us very close together. Somewhere in the genes which the Judge and Aunt Rose had passed on to her were great courage, cheerfulness, and an indomitable will to live. We did not often give up hope, and then only in momentary extravagances we knew we could not afford.

The bad part, for both of us, I think, lay in the technique that was then the only known attack on tuberculosis. The technique was immobilization. The cornerstone of its structured environment was the immobilization of mind and emotions as well as body.

The patient was not only required to lie motionless while the healing tissue formed around the infected lesion. In addition, he must be kept insulated from anything that might stimulate the emotions and hence the heart, which had always the power to drive blood under pressure through the slowly thickening tissues that were sealing in the bacteria. Hence it was necessary to build around the patient a wall strong enough to insulate him from life itself, a wall within which everything was peaceful and serene.

And this of course meant living an unreal life, a life in which conversation must be confined to light anecdote, interesting enough to be diverting, but peopled only with characters from whom the human poisons had been extracted. At Tommy's bedside at Saranac Lake—to which I commuted weekends—my role was Scheherazade's, the teller of endless happy tales the spell of which must never be broken lest the dawn come, the hard dawn of reality in whose clear light it be revealed that there is no one left to hear the tales themselves.

The effect of this Scheherazade role is, I think, that one is drawn irresistibly into this dream world oneself, emotionally at least, in a suspense of human animation. It is a rather lovely world, all healing strength and kindness. It has its gratifications, deep ones. But it is a world as cut off from reality as a schizophrenic's, a world manufactured for a specific beneficent purpose, but still a world that has no real existence beyond one's fantasy.

My life on *The New Yorker* fitted perfectly into my new life with Tommy. Most of these years, with Tommy curing, I lived alone in a two-room flat half a mile from the office. I could literally devote every waking hour to the magazine, and that made Ross as happy as he could be, considering that I was now past my Jesus phase and functioning simply as the practical member of a family of schizophrenics—the one who gets the beds made and something on the table to eat.

The parallel is a good one because any magazine of humor and satire *must* be peopled by schizophrenics who live in fantasy. The unreal is their stock in trade and they are damned to live in some confusion over what is real and what imagined.

Having plenty of fantasy now in what Ross would call my personal life, I had a savage hunger for reality in my work and drove Ross's hapless organization for him with a sarcastic intensity which I am told is still wryly recalled.

The New Yorker per se, demanding as it was, was far from my only contact with reality. Even more demanding was the problem of how to pay for the mounting cost of Tommy's illnesses. During our first year there had been hospital bills and trained nurses to support much of the time Tommy was at home. Nurses cost only fifty-six dollars a week then, but my whole salary wasn't much over twice that. Eventually I was to have a house in Saranac to support and the medical costs were to top ten thousand in a single year.

The first attack I made on this problem was very much in the spirit of the times. Friends of mine—Poly Hooker was one—were getting slaphappy rich in Wall Street; I saw no reason why I shouldn't put the big bull market to the more useful purpose of paying my doctors' bills.

The beginnings of this adventure must have been only a few months after I was married, for the capital with which I went in business was a discreetly given gift from my father-in-law. He and Aunt Rose had come to our tiny two-room flat to dinner, and he had left a thousand-dollar bill—there were such things in the twenties—behind him on the dinner table. He told us about it in the hallway as he left, with a casual "You might find something you'd like to buy with it for your apartment."

What with already having more wedding presents than we knew what to do with, our decision had been to hide this money from ourselves. By the next year, when the pressure began to come on, I had been made vaguely aware that the Judge's current financial operations were in a stock on the big board known as Manhattan Electrical Supply. I would have considered it an impropriety to ask a direct question, but from his conversations at occasional dinners I gathered that he still thought well of it.

So I bought fifty-six hundred dollars' worth of it—one hundred shares at fifty something—with his thousand. That was the way the market ran in the twenties. You put up your ten-point margin and the stock was nominally yours.

By the summer of 1927, my pyramided one thousand dollars was thirty thousand and I was about as confused on the subject of money as I have ever been before or since. Through no efforts of my own, I was almost rich. Six-day weeks of sixteen hours a day on *The New Yorker* netted me no more than a point and a half on a single hundred shares! Moreover, I was being called every hour on the hour by a broker's clerk and was obviously becoming more concerned with the gyrations of Manhattan Electrical Supply than with *The New Yorker's* less spectacular circulation growth.

Also, I now found myself in bed with two hitherto total strangers, Fear and Greed. I was greedy for more and fearful of losing what I had, and acutely unhappy about the whole business.

So when the symptoms of my psychological confusion became too marked to ignore, and I got to where I could hardly tell whether I was thinking about a ticker tape or a "Talk" piece, I had myself up on the carpet and made a decision. It was the magazine, not the market, that I respected; I knew how to make my living on *The New Yorker* and I knew just as clearly that I didn't know one darned thing about what Manhattan Electrical Supply stock was really worth.

I made my decision and I acted on it. I sold however many hundred shares I now had on margin for a cash balance with my broker, and that night, finding myself at my father-in-law's table, I told him for the first time what I had done with the present he

had given us. And when I finished, I also told him that I'd quit
—and why.

I noted that the Judge was silent during my speech, and that
he seemed thoughtful after it. But I had no way of knowing then
that he himself had pyramided a hesitantly extended credit into
several millions of dollars—and was that very week preparing to
lay the whole on the line in one of those bull-versus-bear show-
downs that were the hallmark of predepression markets.

In a military sense, the battle lines were already drawn, the
troops in motion into line. Within the week, from all over the
country there would come selling orders into the market backed
by X millions of his enemies' dollars. These dollars had already
been put up by the bear forces, and they would be met, after a
strategic retreat, by Y millions of buying orders now under the
Judge's control. In the end, one or the other of the forces would
be completely destroyed—the bears trapped in a cornered market
or the bulls broken beyond salvage.

And here was the innocent son-in-law of one of the generals
calmly telling how he had walked out onto the battlefield to
pick daisies! I can see his smile of gentle amusement now—but
the single sentence he had to add was the one that ruined me.
"It's not a good market for you now . . ." he said, hesitating,
"but you might put in an order for a thousand shares at *some*
price—oh, say twenty points below the market . . . just in case
it should sell off." He couldn't quite resist the temptation to add
my squad of dollars to his Order of Battle!

I had faith, if nothing else. I did exactly what the Judge said,
except that to be on the safe side I think I made it thirty points
instead of twenty. The stock was then selling in the one hundred
thirties—up over seventy-five points from where I'd begun. So I
put my supporting order in at one hundred "and forgot about it,"
as the saying goes.

On the day of the catastrophe—it was August 11, 1927—
Manhattan Electric broke from one twenty-one into the fifties in
the last hour before the Exchange suspended trading in it. On the

way down, my thousand shares had been bought as ordered, and forty-five points later they had been sold again. I had lost all of my thirty thousand dollars—and fifteen thousand more. And only the week before, considering my new capital now secure, I had signed a five-year lease on a penthouse apartment at a rental of five thousand a year. Tommy was better, and I was hoping against hope that in cheerful airy surroundings I could keep her that way in New York.

The battle of Manhattan Electrical Supply stock was the last major engagement the Judge ever fought. His financial army was in rout, and at least one ally—in whose name a million dollars' worth of stock had been carried—was to commit suicide as a result. The Judge's own deficit was six or seven million dollars.

This time the creditors took away the house in Bay Shore and even the automobiles. For a while there seemed nothing left, really, except the dream of the suit against the government.

The last night at Bay Shore, the Judge gave a dinner to a dozen of his oldest and closest friends and associates. Tommy and I were there. It was a very gay dinner, with champagne flowing freely. It was all very romantic and almost, but not quite, moving when the Judge rose to announce, "Gentlemen, you've seen me bent but you will never see me broken," and the men clapped and several of the women cried. But there would still be that suicide to explain, and God knows how many thousand anonymous little people who were wiped out.

The day that Manhattan Electrical Supply crashed was a Thursday, and even in my small walk-on role there was a touch of drama—a series of coincidences, had it not been for which I would have gone through it all unscathed. The night before the debacle, the Judge had spent until midnight on the telephone in a last-minute search for new allies, for by that time he knew almost to the hour when his opponents would begin selling.

At 1:00 A.M., having done everything that could be done, he lay sleepless, evaluating the odds, knowing all too well the risks. And lying there, there came back to him the memory of my conversation with him a few weeks before. I had never told him whether I had or had not acted on his advice to support the market. But he knew now that he did not want his daughter and me involved.

The problem, then, was how to warn me. You might have thought that such a simple solution as picking up the telephone would have turned the trick. But in an affair involving so many millions, the Judge took it for granted that his phone was tapped. (He knew so much about his opponents that I am sure he must have tapped theirs.) Nor did he even trust his servants. So he got himself out of bed, dressed, and walked through the night until he found a telegraph office that was open—I think it was on Fifty-ninth Street. From there, he sent a carefully worded telegram advising me to withdraw my buying orders before the market opened.

Knowing that I often left my apartment early to go to the office, the Judge addressed the message to *The New Yorker,* where he also knew that I had a very competent secretary. But what he did not know was that I had had another crisis with my own behavior that week. Psychologically, the thirty thousand in cash at the broker's was burning a hole in my soul as well as my pocket. I found myself still thinking about it, still reading the financial pages when I should have been reading manuscripts. And for the first time that I could remember, I had been formally reproached by Ross for getting behind.

So of all days I had to pick that particular Thursday to stay home from the office in order to catch up. At the office, brokers still called me and there were a thousand routine distractions.

That was coincidence enough, but for the telegram the Judge sent to spend the day unopened on my desk it also required that my perfect secretary had to choose that morning, of all others in the year, to have her hair done. So the telegram that would have saved me a fortune lay unopened under a pile of incoming manuscripts.

And finally, for me to become so inexorably involved, it took my state of mind that morning to refuse to speak on the phone. My broker, who was a friend of mine, did run me down at home in an effort to tell me of rumors about Manhattan Electrical Supply. He got through to me all right—and was on the wire just long enough for me to tell him to go jump in the river. I was trying to write a piece for *The New Yorker* and didn't care what the market did!

When he got through to me again I had been sold out.

The emotion I recall is one of intense relief—for myself. Whatever it cost, it was over and I had really hated it. Then came a sudden appalled consciousness of how the debacle would affect the lives of everyone connected with the Judge's little empire. Southern-style, the Judge had peopled it with his kinfolk. Not many of them ever recovered.

By the next morning, in my own life the light was cool and clear and the weather calm. Unconfused at last, I asked my father for the loan of enough of his capital on which to borrow what I owed from a bank. It took me half a dozen years to get the last of it paid off, but by using my father's collateral I had relieved the pressure and could get back to work.

At that it might have taken me sixty years instead of six had it not been for the indomitable quality of the little financial Napoleon who had just met his Waterloo. I think the thing that hurt most, in the week after it was all over, was having to break the news to him that my rowboat, too, had gone down with the fleet. Until I told him, he had presumed that his midnight telegram had at least saved Tommy and me. It was a month after that that he came to me with what was at once a typically romantic story and an unusually practical proposition.

This was the romantic story: Many years before I had married his daughter, Carden had done a financial favor for a rich man. His friend had wanted to settle the account—to pay off, as it were —but the Judge had refused. The favor had cost him nothing and the man was his friend. So the friend had taken Aunt Rose to one side and given her, without the Judge's knowledge, a sealed envelope with her name on it. "Rose," he said, "I have known your husband all my life. One of these days he will need this."

Rose understood. She had hidden the envelope somewhere all those years. The week after the crash she found it, and inside were three ten-thousand-dollar bills.

These I have had in my hands, because the proposition the Judge made me involved turning them over to me to operate for him under my name. With every other asset attached, and his debts involving years of negotiation, this thirty thousand dollars of Aunt Rose's was the only chance he had to come back. For the first time in his life, the loss of a battle had cost him even his creditors' confidence.

The proposition the Judge made to me was that I should open brokerage accounts in my name and he would tell me what to buy or sell—for Aunt Rose's account. If we lost, that was the end of it; if we won, I was to get ten per cent of the profits.

It was a sporting proposition, and those three ten-thousand-dollar bills in five years became one and a half million dollars. The Judge was that good. I forget how much I took out on my percentage—in the end enough to pay what I had lost in Manhattan Electrical Supply plus what it eventually took to get Tommy well. Once those two objectives seemed accomplished, I gave our little business back to the Judge. He was way out ahead —several hundred thousand dollars by that time, I think—but he was now gambling with such large amounts that it was impossible for me to forget Manhattan Electrical Supply. With everything in my name, if there were to be another crash, I felt it really would be the end of me.

My decision was respected, and we parted in business good friends. During the years the Judge operated through me, there was a hard, cautious quality to his thinking. I don't recall a single investment—and we made literally hundreds—that did not in the end come out well, because it was based on the clearest of analyses and the soundest of timing.

But I had been right in my basic judgment of the Judge's personality. A year after we dissolved our partnership, he became convinced that there would be a bad crop year in wheat and that the price would skyrocket. He was rich enough by then to send a dozen scouts out personally to report to him from the field. He had every available figure in hand—and he bet the whole million and a half he now had on his judgment.

He was absolutely and spectacularly right concerning an impending shortage of grain in the United States, and on the limit of supplies available elsewhere in the free world. The only trouble was, the year he chose to analyze was the very year in which the custodians of the Soviet Socialist Republics' grain bins chose to dump their surplus on the free market!

Soviet grain had never been included in his, or anyone else's, statistics. For years the Russians had had none to export. Their sudden shift in policy broke the grain market and George A. Carden for the last time.

But the Judge's toast had been the truth—at least his spirit was never broken. Until his death, in his late seventies, he remained as confident of his destiny as ever. He had even taken up the practice of law again to provide himself with the capital for one last challenge.

xx · Gentlemen Pranksters All

I doubt if any of my associates at *The New Yorker* knew of these turbulent events—certainly not Ross, because we were no longer on a personal basis. Everybody knew about Tommy's illness—I don't mean that. But the obstacles that had to be overcome to survive it, these were my own business, and my only confidant was my friend Bishop, now a young doctor in his famous father's office.

My closest friends on *The New Yorker* were Jim Thurber and

Andy White. The most fun I had was with Andy. We used to amuse ourselves by thinking up pranks that might make *New Yorker* pieces—like the time we organized ourselves into an expedition to explore the headwaters of the Bronx River. It flowed down through the suburbs in plain view of commuters on passing trains, but not even the biggest atlas had anything to say about whence it came.

So Andy got a canoe from some place, lashed it to the top of his car, and we sallied forth to find out. Obviously an Indian guide was indicated, so we got hold of a department-store dummy, bought him an Indian fright wig, and dressed him in costume; ourselves we rigged as trappers.

We got our expedition waterborne somewhere in the vicinity of Mount Vernon, just late enough in the afternoon so that the commuting trains, disgorging home-bound suburbanites, might provide an audience to cheer us on our way.

And indeed they did, as we paddled happily along—until someone tipped off the State Police. We found these uniformed officers remarkably uninterested in the scientific purposes of our journey, but there was nothing in their manuals that specifically prohibited exploration. They had to resort to a threatened charge of disturbing the peace to stop us. This was demonstrably fraudulent because the only thing we were disturbing was the settled habits of the suburbanites, now packed three or four deep along the shores of the river, letting their dinners get cold while they waited to find out what the devil it was all about.

We tried to explain to the law that this was, in our opinion, a good thing in the lives of suburbanites, who were often the cause of unnecessary wars instigated solely for the purpose of relieving the monotony of their lives. But all in vain; out we were yanked.

Once, on a similar quest for knowledge, we overdid things a bit. This was when a saleman who tried to sell Andy a burial plot in a new cemetery gave us the idea of inviting a crematorium salesman to compete with him for our mortal remains. We were sure their competitive arguments would make a hilarious piece.

But midway in the crematorium fellow's too-graphic description of the indignities involved in embalming, Andy found himself turning pale green and had to retire to the solace of a lavatory. This is the only time I know that E. B. White even tried to emulate Evelyn Waugh.

Really our best lark was with John S. Sumner and his N.Y. Society for the Suppression of Vice. It all began when a Greenwich Village wag pinched the sign from the Society's headquarters on Twelfth Street, appropriating it to his use as a cocktail tray. Someone told me the story; I verified and printed it in "Talk." Thereupon the great John S. descended on *The New Yorker*'s office in person waving subpoenas accompanied by demands that I reveal the source of my information so that he could recover his stolen property.

This was everybody's meat and nobody's poison because Sumner's society was a favorite butt of *The New Yorker*'s, and here he was delivering himself into our hands with a clear-cut challenge to our journalistic ethics. It was agreed that a few months in jail for me was a small price to pay for our honor—and the incidental publicity.

But we must have been a little too eager, for the canny Mr. Sumner backed down and offered to settle for reimbursement of the cost of a new sign. This seemed reasonable but involved loss of face—so Andy and Jim and I retreated to a speak-easy to consider our next move. I can't remember who came up with the idea—Andy, probably; he had the better classical education. Our answer was to use the Trojan horse technique.

Sumner's sign, which had been turned over to us as a token of the thief's appreciation, was a heavy wooden plaque about three by five feet square with the title "N.Y. Society for the Suppression of Vice" blocked out in gold lettering against an ingenious background of black paint finely sanded to give it texture. It was quite an unusual job.

We asked Mr. Sumner if a replica would serve his purpose; and he agreed. We then had the replica made—but with a false front, so that the panel with the lettering on it could be removed to reveal a scantily dressed chorus girl kicking off Mr. Sumner's stovepipe hat. A cabinetmaker on Third Avenue did the job for us, and one of *The New Yorker* artists painted the caricature. After formal presentation to the Society, we expected that the sign would be bolted back on the façade of its headquarters. Next night the false front was to be removed and a friendly press invited to take photographs of *The New Yorker*'s own version. Let Mr. Sumner *then* put me in jail for contempt; we would laugh him out of town.

All this might very well have come to pass had not the once-burned Mr. Sumner now bolted his sign to the building way up between its second-story windows, well beyond the reach of any pranksters not on stilts.

This *really* put it up to us, and it took Andy and me three separate attempts to get the job done.

The first idea we came up with was that we should disguise ourselves as painters carrying a ladder. We did and nobody stopped us in our invasion of Twelfth Street. But with me holding the ladder and Andy just reaching the top rung, the window alongside the sign was abruptly flung open and an irate head demanded to know what we were doing. We made it back around the corner, ladder and all, at full gallop.

We now reasoned that the whole block would be alerted to bogus painters; but the one thing New Yorkers *never* notice is the utterly bizarre; so we thought we should try that. Instead of disguising ourselves as something plausible, we should go to the other extreme. So for our next foray Andy rented a bright-red fireman's suit, complete with an antique helmet, and I put on a shiny top hat and wore white tie and tails.

And, by golly, our reasoning was sound! In the clear light of a late summer evening, with the street well populated with passers-by, no one paid the least attention to us. Again up went our ladder and up went Fireman White—only, this time, to run into mechanical difficulties. The blankety-blank false panel wouldn't come off! To conceal its existence, it had been set in a frame, one strip of which was nailed too securely in place. For half an hour we went up and down that ladder to wrestle with it—until from his second-story vantage point Andy was the first to perceive a uniformed patrolman rounding the corner from Sixth Avenue half a block away. It was too much to expect *him* to be incurious—and that was the end of that.

The final and successful assault came quickly. With our own honor now seriously involved, Andy simply bought a hatchet in a hardware store (to chop away the frame) and went back and did the job in plain clothes in thirty seconds, racing thence to a corner drugstore to tip off the papers.

I am sorry to have to report that the results were an anticlimax. The stupid press sent reporters instead of cameramen. Their presence alerted Mr. Sumner, and he got the sign down before their cameramen could follow up. So we had to be content with the story told in words—which was a great disappointment. Nor did Mr. Sumner fall for the bait and try a second time to bring us into court, which might have made it possible for us to insist that he introduce the naughty sign itself as evidence.

In most of our high jinks, Jim Thurber was a silent collaborator, but in one he played a leading role. His was the whole idea for the Sitting Bull hoax. This one got rolling when Jim picked up the news that a friend of one of my female reporters was on the entertainment committee of the New York Junior League— that happiest of targets for *The New Yorker*'s Helen Hokinson.

The reporter blessed with this august connection was a girl named Haydie Eames, a younger sister of the great Emma Eames. Haydie was quite a character herself. She had swarthy coloring and the hawklike features of a handsome Indian brave, and once upon a time she had been a professional rodeo rider. Actually, Haydie was the first reporter I ever had on the "Talk of the Town" department, and she got the job when she applied for it on a day when I was in a particularly bad humor. I told her first that I wouldn't discuss the matter until she had written some pieces for me. When she entered the counter-argument that, having only just arrived in town, she didn't know anything to write about, I snapped back, "Any damned fool can get a 'Talk' piece by standing on the corner of Forty-fifth Street and Sixth Avenue for fifteen minutes."

Two hours later Haydie was back to turn in a workable piece about a drunken traffic cop in a speak-easy.

"Where the devil did you get that?" I asked.

"Where you said," was her reply, "on the corner of Forty-fifth Street and Sixth Avenue. I asked the traffic cop to buy me a drink—and he did."

Haydie's physical resemblance to a young Indian squaw, plus her connection with the Junior League's entertainment committee, sparked a combustible chamber in Thurber's brain. By the time they took me in on the plot it had been announced in the Junior League's bulletin that on the coming Thursday they would be addressed by none other than Sitting Bull's daughter.

At this point, Andy was requisitioned to write the speech, and his refinement was a script that began as a light satire on the in-tellectual fare offered female culture groups, with the burlesque gradually becoming broader and broader until, toward the end, it was clearly slapstick. The more alert minds in the audience were supposed to catch on about midway through; the first snickers were to break out soon after, and at the end Haydie was to pull off her Indian fright wig and everyone could enjoy a good laugh.

We got the first news that something had gone wrong with *this* gag late in the afternoon on which the lecture had been held. A breathless Haydie came running in to where we waited to get news of her success, screaming "Hide me, hide me—and take this," forthwith proffering us a handbag bulging with greenbacks.

The audience, she presently explained, instead of seeing through Andy's delicate satire, had taken it straight. Andy's pitiful description of life in Sitting Bull's tepee (*Did you know that you can't even hang a picture on the wall of a tepee?*) had reduced the audience to tears. At the end of the speech, some kindhearted Hokinson subject had suggested taking up a collection, and there it was in front of us, hundreds of dollars of loot.

It was I who had to dig them all out of that one, for Haydie was terrified that her friend on the entertainment committee would be expelled from the Junior League. And her friend was a "nice" girl, not a Bohemian like Haydie.

She wasn't expelled, because I took the money back to the Junior League myself, and its appalled officers agreed with me that the less said about the incident the better.

Innocent days!

XXI · And I Did

This same Haydie Eames of the Sitting Bull story dropped in on me a few years after both of us had left *The New Yorker* and said she couldn't get over how much I had changed—not just by taking on twenty or thirty pounds, but even in the way I talked, in my whole attitude toward life, in fact.

"Why, you're almost human now," she volunteered. "On *The New Yorker,* you were disgusted with yourself if you ever said anything nice to anybody. All of you were."

I have no real quarrel with Haydie's picture of those times as I remember them. Toward the end of my years with *The New Yorker,* when my own life had at last begun to stabilize, I came to my own conclusions about Ross's career. I remember well the foundation of my decision to leave him—which was my feeling that his future was already behind him.

In the beginning I had been certain that he was the most brilliantly creative man I would ever meet. The fact that the technique of his creation confused people had nothing to do with the facts. So what if he could articulate only what he did *not* like? That was still a valid way of going about creation; after all, a sculptor's method with marble is no different. He chips away the stone he doesn't want until the image he has somewhere in his subconscious emerges and is left.

Also, I knew many things about the creative part of Ross of which my contemporaries might have been ignorant. During the almost endless hours we spent together the first two years I was with him, he outlined—backward, as usual, tearing down what he was against—half a dozen other new kinds of publications. When we had put over *The New Yorker,* we were going to start some of them.

Ross was still ambitious then. He was going to get on with life just as soon as he could fight his way through the miasma of incompetence and cross-purpose and fatheadedness in which he felt himself immersed. "That God-damned Fleischmann . . . that God-damned Hanrahan . . . those God-damned incompetent bastards that are all we have to get out this magazine with. Women and children, women and children!"

Ross was a Laocoön figure, struggling to be free of the invisible snakes which he thought of as strangling him. But then, even despite the snakes, he did it. There got to be a publication which, if it still failed to please him, was at least an approximation of what he had had in mind.

But instead of going on to launch other ventures—instead of at least attempting to build on his experience with *The New Yorker* to fulfill one of his other dreams—Ross seemed to me to be retreating. The more successful *The New Yorker,* the greater became his anxiety about it. As an individual, he seemed to shrink in stature with success.

It was as if he had become suddenly and prematurely an old man, interested only in preserving and perfecting what was now capable of only a minimum of refinement.

A decade later, when I turned back to Ross in the hope of enlisting him in a project to create a new kind of newspaper, I confirmed it. Many of my own ideas dated back to his own early arguments on the sins of modern journalism. But now I could strike no spark.

Ross wished me well; once when I was at an impasse in my efforts to raise the money, he even went to work for me ably and unasked. But what I wanted more than help in finding a financial backer was the kind of savagely constructive impatience with the *status quo* that I had remembered when he had been creating *The New Yorker.* And this was gone.

Toward my new adventure, I found Ross shy to the point of diffidence and his answer to an invitation to collaborate— or to take over—was that he had his hands full with *The New Yorker.* Things there were worse than ever. It was the same old story I knew so well. He was still at the mercy of women and children and incompetents. Did I realize that it now took a dozen paid employees to handle the simple routine of my old job? I had no idea what he'd been through. . . .

And he meant every word of it, although *The New Yorker* was by then ten deep in talent and had first call on anything written or drawn in its field in the whole continent. Its stockholders were long since millionaires. Ross was still in his forties, but in my eyes he was already a crotchety oldster, as his bête noire, *Time,* would have put it.

These things I felt about Ross when my own crises of the twenties were passed and I could again think of the future. On *The New Yorker* I was long since an old, old old-timer; the excitement of its creation was over and the leadership I had felt in Ross had evaporated.

It was about that time, and in that state of mind, that I received my first overture from Harry Luce's organization. They were starting a new kind of magazine; it was called *Fortune* and it was no further along than *The New Yorker* had been that first morning I'd gone to see Ross.

I said to myself, "I think I'll take a crack at that one."

And I did.

POSTSCRIPT

All the characters in this book are, of course, real—both the living and the dead. But I have chosen to change a few of their names. This I have done whenever I felt that I might cause embarrassment—as, for instance, in my story of the presently distinguished executive whom I once helped so successfully to crib his way through college. I have also used fictitious names to get around the stigma of kiss-and-tell narratives. It doesn't really matter much to the casual reader whether the girl concerned was named Mary or Jane, but it might disturb a lineal descendant, and for what purpose? The episodes involved are hardly historic.

Otherwise, I have done my best to be literally accurate and, whenever possible, to check my memory against what facts are of record. It was Mark Twain, naturally, who made the ultimate comment on autobiographical material when he remarked that it was not the happenings he forgot that bothered him, but the things he remembered so vividly that had not happened at all! In writing this book, I've come to know exactly what he meant. I hereby extend a blanket apology to cover any unintentional lapses.

And, finally, this book is signed Ralph *McAllister* Ingersoll because that's the name my family gave me. For most of my adult life, I've used a shorter signature, without the McAllister part. A speculative press once commented on this omission, hazarding the opinion that I was using the stripped-down version as a personal expression of social protest. Not so. I had simply got tired of having to repeat so many words and capitals in a name that I had to sign so often—as an editor and publisher—on everything from company checks to circulation solicitations. Besides, there are too many ways in which McAllister can be misspelled.

The title of this autobiography, as such, is literal. It is in my mind that one day, God willing, I shall go farther on the voyage, sailing through the years I spent with Harry Luce as the Managing Editor of his *Fortune* magazine and—later—as an august Vice-President and General Manager of his Time, Incorporated during the years that the old *Life* was killed and the new *Life* born.

After that—I dream—could come the fabulous story of *PM*, the "new kind of daily newspaper" once published in the City of New York. It could be fun putting it on paper—and it would lead into still another volume covering the years I spent as a

soldier in the Army of the United States, the more personal side
of those experiences that nudged me to write *The Battle Is the
Pay-off* and *Top Secret*.

Since those years, I've turned my hand to raising a family
and publishing more orthodox newspapers than *PM*—eminently
in that order. And now, when I've turned sixty, people ask me,
curiously, what the whole business has taught me; what, if anything? Should I write another book to still them? Alas, its title
already belongs to someone else—for obviously it would cry out
to be called "Point of No Return"!

But I would not know the answer to that question anyway.
It still is now, as it was in the beginning, a tossup to me whether
life is more fun to live or to write about.